Terraform Associate Certification Exam

350 Questions for Guaranteed Success

1st Edition

www.versatileread.com

Document Control

Proposal Name	:	Terraform Associate Certification Exam: 350 Questions for Guaranteed Success
Document Edition	:	1st
Document Release Date	:	6th August 2024
Reference	:	TCA
VR Product Code	:	20242702TCA

Feedback:

If you have any comments regarding the quality of this book or otherwise alter it to better suit your needs, you can contact us through email at info@versatileread.com

Please make sure to include the book's title and ISBN in your message.

VERSAtile Reads

Voice of the Customer: Thank you for choosing this VersatileRead.com product! We highly value your feedback and insights via email to info@versatileread.com. As a token of appreciation, an amazing discount for your next purchase will be sent in response to your email.

About the Contributors:

Nouman Ahmed Khan

AWS/Azure/GCP-Architect, CCDE, CCIEx5 (R&S, SP, Security, DC, Wireless), CISSP, CISA, CISM, CRISC, ISO27K-LA is a Solution Architect working with a global telecommunication provider. He works with enterprises, mega-projects, and service providers to help them select the best-fit technology solutions. He also works as a consultant to understand customer business processes and helps select an appropriate technology strategy to support business goals. He has more than eighteen years of experience working with global clients. One of his notable experiences was his tenure with a large managed security services provider, where he was responsible for managing the complete MSSP product portfolio. With his extensive knowledge and expertise in various areas of technology, including cloud computing, network infrastructure, security, and risk management, Nouman has become a trusted advisor for his clients.

Abubakar Saeed

Abubakar Saeed is a trailblazer in the realm of technology and innovation. With a rich professional journey spanning over twenty-nine years, Abubakar has seamlessly blended his expertise in engineering with his passion for transformative leadership. Starting humbly at the grassroots level, he has significantly contributed to pioneering the Internet in Pakistan and beyond. Abubakar's multifaceted experience encompasses managing, consulting, designing, and implementing projects, showcasing his versatility as a leader.

His exceptional skills shine in leading businesses, where he champions innovation and transformation. Abubakar stands as a testament to the power of visionary leadership, heading operations, solutions design, and integration. His emphasis on adhering to project timelines and exceeding customer expectations has set him apart as a great leader. With an unwavering commitment to adopting technology for operational simplicity and enhanced efficiency, Abubakar Saeed continues to inspire and drive change in the industry.

Dr. Fahad Abdali

Dr. Fahad Abdali is an esteemed leader with an outstanding twenty-year track record in managing diverse businesses. With a stellar educational background, including a bachelor's degree from the prestigious NED University of Engineers & Technology and a Ph.D. from the University of Karachi, Dr. Abdali epitomizes academic excellence and continuous professional growth.

Dr. Abdali's leadership journey is marked by his unwavering commitment to innovation and his astute understanding of industry dynamics. His ability to navigate intricate challenges has driven growth and nurtured organizational triumph. Driven by a passion for excellence, he stands as a beacon of inspiration within the business realm. With his remarkable leadership skills, Dr. Fahad Abdali continues to steer businesses toward unprecedented success, making him a true embodiment of a great leader.

Arshamah Sheikh

Arshamah Sheikh is a seasoned content developer with extensive expertise in cloud computing, IT infrastructure, information security, database management, cybersecurity, and Microsoft technologies. She holds certifications in Cisco's NDG Linux Unhatched, Database Design, and Cloud Solution Architecture. With her deep knowledge and professional qualifications, Arshamah excels in creating intuitive, visually appealing content that effectively communicates complex technical concepts.

Table of Contents

About Terraform Associate Certification

What is DevOps?

DevOps is a term derived from combining "Development" and "Operations." It represents a collaborative approach where software development (Dev) and IT operations (Ops) teams work together to conceive, build, and deliver software rapidly and securely. Originating from Agile methodologies, DevOps enhances speed through automation, collaboration, feedback, and iterative improvements. It signifies a cultural shift in IT practices, emphasizing incremental development and rapid delivery while fostering a shared responsibility for achieving business outcomes. By integrating Agile and lean principles, DevOps creates a culture of accountability and improved collaboration, aiming to enhance the flow and value delivery of applications across the development lifecycle.

What is Infrastructure as Code?

Infrastructure as code (IaC) fundamentally transforms how computing infrastructure is managed by leveraging code to automate provisioning, configuration, and management tasks. Traditionally, setting up and maintaining infrastructure components like servers, networks, and databases involved manual processes prone to errors and inefficiencies, particularly as applications scale. IaC addresses these challenges by allowing developers and operations teams to define infrastructure configurations through code. This approach ensures consistency and repeatability across environments, streamlines deployment processes, and reduces the time and effort spent on manual tasks. By automating infrastructure management, IaC enables organizations to achieve greater agility, scalability, and reliability in their IT operations, empowering teams to focus more on innovation and delivering value to customers rather than managing infrastructure intricacies manually.

Evolution from Traditional Infrastructure to Infrastructure as Code (IaC) with Terraform

The evolution from traditional infrastructure management to Infrastructure as Code (IaC) with Terraform signifies a shift towards automated, programmable provisioning and configuration of IT resources. Instead of manual setups prone to errors, Terraform's declarative approach using HCL allows for efficient, consistent deployment and scaling of infrastructure across various environments. This approach supports agile practices, ensures reliability through version control, and enhances operational efficiency through automation.

Introduction to Terraform

Terraform is an open-source infrastructure as code (IaC) tool developed by HashiCorp. It allows users to define and manage their infrastructure using a declarative configuration language, such as HashiCorp Configuration Language (HCL) or JSON. The primary purpose of Terraform is to automate the provisioning, configuration, and management of infrastructure resources across various cloud providers (like AWS, Azure, and Google Cloud) and on-premises environments. By defining infrastructure as code, Terraform enables users to specify the desired state of their infrastructure in configuration files, which Terraform then interprets and executes to achieve and maintain that desired state efficiently. This approach helps organizations achieve consistency, repeatability, and scalability in their infrastructure deployments while also facilitating collaboration and version control practices similar to software development workflows.

Benefits of Using Terraform

- Terraform enables infrastructure management through code, allowing for versioning and collaborative development similar to application code.
- It automates the provisioning and management of infrastructure resources, reducing manual errors and enhancing operational efficiency.

- Terraform supports managing infrastructure across multiple cloud providers concurrently, facilitating flexible multi-cloud strategies.
- Ensures consistent infrastructure configurations across different environments (e.g., development, staging, production), reducing configuration drift.
- Facilitates scaling of infrastructure resources up or down as needed, supporting dynamic business requirements.
- Promotes modular architecture through reusable modules, enhancing code reuse and standardization across projects.
- Manages infrastructure state with a state file, enabling accurate tracking and incremental updates to infrastructure resources.

Key Components in Terraform

Key components in Terraform include:

- **Variables**: Used to customize Terraform configurations by passing values.
- **Provider**: Plugins that interface with APIs to manage resources.
- **Module**: Organizes Terraform configurations into reusable units.
- **State**: Stores the current state and metadata of managed resources.
- **Resources**: Blocks defining infrastructure components to be managed.
- **Data Sources**: Retrieves information about existing infrastructure.
- **Output Values**: Expose specific information from a module to other parts of the configuration.
- **Plan**: Determines the actions to achieve the desired infrastructure state.
- **Apply**: Executes changes to reach the desired state as per the plan.

Terraform Architecture

Terraform's architecture is designed to simplify managing infrastructure using code. It relies on configuration files written in HCL (HashiCorp Configuration Language), where you define resources, providers, variables, and outputs. The Terraform CLI provides commands like `terraform init` to set up your project, `terraform plan` to preview changes, `terraform apply` to make those changes, and `terraform destroy` to remove resources.

Providers, specified in your configuration, let Terraform interact with cloud platforms like AWS or Azure. Terraform keeps track of your infrastructure's current state, either locally or in remote storage like AWS S3 or Terraform Cloud. It uses a dependency graph to understand dependencies between resources and executes changes in a planned sequence to ensure your infrastructure is managed accurately and reliably.

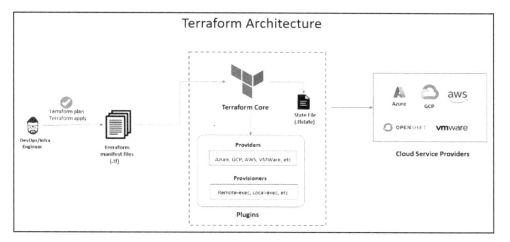

Core Concepts of Terraform

The core concept of terraform

- **Declarative Configuration:** Terraform uses HCL (HashiCorp Configuration Language) to define infrastructure as code (IaC), specifying the desired end-state of resources.
- **Terraform State Management:** It maintains a state file (`terraform.tfstate`) to track the current state of deployed resources, facilitating future updates and resource management.
- **Providers and Modules:** Providers are plugins enabling Terraform to interact with various infrastructure platforms, while modules facilitate reusable and modular configurations.
- **Infrastructure as Code (IaC):** Terraform automates infrastructure management through code, ensuring consistency, scalability, and efficiency in deployments.

- **Execution Plans:** Terraform generates execution plans (`terraform plan`) showing anticipated changes before applying them, aiding in validation and risk assessment.
- **Resource Graph:** It constructs a dependency graph of resources based on configuration, enabling Terraform to determine the correct sequence of resource provisioning and updates.
- **State Locking:** Terraform supports state locking to prevent concurrent access issues, ensuring the integrity and consistency of the state file during collaborative environments

Terraform Lifecycle

Terraform operates through a series of key commands and processes that manage infrastructure as code efficiently:

Terraform init

- Initializes the working directory containing Terraform configuration files (*.tf).
- Downloads necessary provider plugins.
- Initializes the backend to store the Terraform state.

Terraform plan

- Generates an execution plan to achieve the desired state defined in the configuration files (*.tf).
- Compares the current state with the desired state.
- Outputs a detailed plan of actions (create, update, delete) without making any changes to real infrastructure.

Terraform apply

- Executes the actions proposed in the execution plan to modify real infrastructure.
- Prompts for confirmation before making any changes.
- Applies changes sequentially to create, update, or delete resources as defined in the plan.

VERSAtile Reads

Terraform destroy

- Deletes all resources managed by Terraform.
- Generates a destruction plan showing which resources will be deleted.
- Prompts for confirmation before executing destruction.
- Removes resources in reverse order of their creation to handle dependencies properly.

Roles and Responsibilities of Terraform Certified Associate

- Design and plan infrastructure using Terraform to meet project requirements.
- Implement Terraform configurations to provision and manage cloud resources effectively.
- Apply Terraform best practices to ensure reliable and secure infrastructure deployments.
- Collaborate with teams to align infrastructure provisioning with development goals.
- Manage version control and Terraform state to maintain infrastructure consistency.
- Develop reusable Terraform modules for efficient infrastructure provisioning.
- Automate infrastructure deployment and configuration using Terraform scripts and CI/CD pipelines.
- Troubleshoot and debug Terraform configurations and infrastructure issues effectively.
- Continuously evaluate and enhance infrastructure design for improved performance.
- Stay updated with the latest Terraform features and best practices for effective infrastructure management.

Skills Required for Terraform Certification

These foundational skills are essential for effectively using Terraform to manage and automate infrastructure deployments across both on-premises and cloud environments.

- **Basic Terminal Skills:** Proficiency in navigating, manipulating files, and executing commands in a terminal environment.
- **Understanding of On-Premises Architecture:** Familiarity with traditional on-premises infrastructure setups and configurations.
- **Understanding of Cloud Architecture:** Knowledge of cloud computing principles, including virtualization, networking, and storage concepts.

What is the Terraform Associate certification?

The Terraform Associate certification is a credential that verifies proficiency in utilizing Terraform for managing infrastructure as code (IaC) across diverse cloud and on-premises environments. This certification validates an individual's ability to effectively deploy, manage, and update infrastructure resources using Terraform's declarative configuration language, HCL (HashiCorp Configuration Language). Holders of this certification demonstrate competence in defining infrastructure requirements, automating resource provisioning, and ensuring infrastructure consistency and scalability. By earning the Terraform Associate certification, professionals establish their credibility in leveraging Terraform to streamline operations, adopt DevOps practices, and support modern cloud-native architectures.

Why Pursue Terraform Associate Certification?

Pursuing Terraform certification is a strategic career move, affirming expertise in infrastructure automation through managing infrastructure as code (IaC) across diverse environments. This certification enhances credibility and unlocks opportunities in roles such as Terraform administrator or DevOps engineer, which is critical in modern IT environments. It ensures mastery of Terraform's declarative configuration language (HCL), vital for efficient resource provisioning and scalability. Additionally, certification demonstrates a commitment to staying updated with industry best practices, equipping professionals to meet the increasing demand for cloud-native infrastructure management solutions. Overall, terraform certification validates skills and prepares individuals for growth in a dynamic technology landscape.

Benefits of Terraform Certification

- Certification validates proficiency in Terraform, demonstrating the ability to effectively manage infrastructure as code (IaC) across cloud and on-premises environments.
- Enhances credibility and marketability, opening doors to roles such as Terraform administrator, DevOps engineer, or cloud infrastructure specialist.
- Provides structured learning and ensures mastery of Terraform's declarative configuration language (HCL) and best practices.
- Demonstrates commitment to staying current with industry standards and trends in infrastructure automation and cloud computing.
- Increases employability in organizations adopting or transitioning to cloud-native architectures and DevOps practices.
- Positions professionals for leadership roles in managing scalable and efficient infrastructure deployments using Terraform.
- Access to a global community of Terraform practitioners and resources for continuous learning and collaboration.

Certified Terraform Associate Exam Format

The exam lasts for 60 minutes and consists of multiple-choice Drag and drag-and-drop case studies and multiple responses, which will be discussed in more detail later. A passing score of 70% is required.

Exam Information

Terraform Associate Certification

Prior Certification Not Required	**Exam Validity** 2 Years
Exam Fee $70.5 USD	**Exam Duration** 60 Minutes
No. of Questions 57-60 Questions	**Passing Marks** 70% or Above
Recommended Experience Basic understanding of On premises & cloud architecture	
Exam Format Multiple Choice, Drag & drop, Case studies, Multiple response	

Key Focus Area

Infrastructure as Code (IaC) Concepts

- Understand the principles of IaC for maintaining infrastructure through code.

Terraform's Purpose vs. Other IaC Tools

- Differentiate Terraform's role in orchestrating multi-cloud infrastructure compared to other IaC tools.

Terraform Basics

- Master the fundamentals of Terraform, including HCL syntax, providers, resources, variables, outputs, and modules.

Using the Terraform CLI

- Utilize Terraform CLI commands for initializing, planning, applying, and destroying infrastructure resources.

Interacting with Terraform Modules

- Effectively integrate and reuse Terraform modules to simplify and modularize infrastructure configuration.

Navigating Terraform Workflow

- Manage Terraform workflow phases, including initialization, planning, applying changes, and destroying resources.

Implementing and Maintaining State

- Implement best practices for managing Terraform state files to track infrastructure configuration and changes.

Terraform Cloud and Enterprise Capabilities

- Explore advanced features of Terraform Cloud and Enterprise for collaboration, governance, and automation in large-scale deployments.

Preparation Tips

To excel in your exam preparation and ensure a successful outcome, consider the following strategies:

- Emphasize hands-on practice for a solid understanding of concepts.
- Use Google and Stack Overflow for troubleshooting if you encounter issues.
- Take notes while learning to enhance retention.
- Create 1-2 small projects using Terraform to gain practical experience.
- Share your learning journey publicly to engage with the community and gain insights.

Future of Terraform and DevOps

In the fast-changing world of technology, Terraform and DevOps are experiencing significant growth. They are revolutionizing how infrastructure is managed and automated, enabling efficient and scalable deployment of resources to meet the demands of modern applications effectively.

- **Increased Adoption:** Terraform continues to be widely adopted across industries due to its ability to automate infrastructure provisioning across multi-cloud and hybrid-cloud environments.
- **Enhanced Integrations:** Integration with other DevOps tools and platforms such as Kubernetes, CI/CD pipelines, and configuration management systems like Ansible and Chef enhances its versatility and adoption.
- **Evolving Features:** HashiCorp, the creator of Terraform, regularly updates the tool with new features, improvements, and support for emerging cloud services and infrastructure needs.
- **Infrastructure as Code (IaC) Standard:** As IaC becomes standard practice, Terraform's declarative syntax and state management capabilities make it a preferred choice for infrastructure automation.
- **Community and Ecosystem Growth:** A vibrant community contributes modules and best practices and supports knowledge sharing, ensuring Terraform remains relevant and adaptable to evolving infrastructure demands.

- **Focus on Security and Compliance:** Continued emphasis on security features, compliance controls, and governance capabilities ensures Terraform remains aligned with enterprise requirements.
- **Cloud-Native Solutions:** Integration with cloud-native solutions and services further expands Terraform's utility in managing dynamic and scalable cloud infrastructures.

Demand for TCA In 2024

The demand for the Terraform Certified Associate (TCA) certification is expected to remain strong in 2024 for several reasons:

- **Industry Recognition:** The TCA certification, developed by HashiCorp, is globally recognized and vendor-neutral, demonstrating proficiency in managing infrastructure as code (IaC) across various environments.
- **Career Advancement:** Achieving TCA certification can lead to significant career growth, opening doors to roles such as DevOps Engineer, Cloud Engineer, and Infrastructure Engineer, often with higher salaries and responsibilities.
- **Skill Validation:** The TCA exam is performance-based, testing practical skills through real-world tasks, ensuring certified professionals are well-prepared to manage infrastructure using Terraform.
- **Increasing Terraform Adoption:** With the rise of multi-cloud strategies and scalable infrastructure needs, demand for skilled Terraform professionals is growing. Terraform automates infrastructure deployment, management, and scaling, making it crucial in modern IT.

Practice Questions

Consider that VERSAtileOptic is a leading digital security product for enterprises, providing cybersecurity for hybrid cloud environments. Contact us for continuous security assessment and compliance monitoring. Secure your IT by knowing your CyberExposure Index and prioritizing emerging threats with our Threat Contextualization engine.

1. What does integrating Infrastructure as Code (IaC) into CI/CD pipelines primarily automate?

A. Code testing
B. Code deployment
C. Provisioning and configuration of infrastructure
D. All of the above

2. Which organization has benefited from fully automated deployment pipelines?

A. TechWorld Services
B. VERSAtileOptic Solutions
C. DevOps Inc.
D. InfraTech Solutions

3. What has the integration of IaC into CI/CD pipelines reduced for organizations?

A. Development time
B. Manual interventions
C. Code quality
D. Deployment frequency

4. Where can community-contributed modules for Terraform be found?

A. GitHub

B. Docker Hub

C. Terraform Registry

D. Ansible Galaxy

5. Which type of projects enrich the IaC ecosystem?

A. Proprietary software

B. Closed source projects

C. Open-source projects

D. Commercial products

6. What types of pre-built solutions accelerate the adoption of Infrastructure as Code (IaC)?

A. Docker containers

B. Virtual machines

C. Ansible Playbooks

D. Kubernetes clusters

7. Which of the following is not listed as a benefit of Infrastructure as Code (IaC) in CI/CD pipelines?

A. Increased deployment speed

B. Enhanced infrastructure security

C. Reduced manual interventions

D. Access to community contributions

8. When using Terraform with cloud providers like AWS or Azure, what is the primary role of a Terraform provider?

A. To define and manage Terraform state

B. To authenticate and authorize API requests

C. To provision and manage infrastructure resources

D. To store and manage sensitive credentials

9. What is the primary benefit of community contributions to the IaC ecosystem?

A. Reduced software licensing costs
B. Enhanced technical support
C. Availability of pre-built solutions and best practices
D. Increased marketing reach

10. Which of the following statements is true about the landscape of IaC?

A. It is dominated by proprietary software.
B. It lacks significant community contributions.
C. It is rich with community contributions and open-source projects.
D. It is a new and emerging field with limited resources.

11. What is the primary function of Terraform's state file?

A. To store backups of configuration files
B. To reflect the real-time status of resources
C. To manage user permissions
D. To log error messages

12. What benefit does maintaining a state file provide in Terraform?

A. Enhanced user interface
B. Performance optimizations and precise control over infrastructure changes
C. Improved security
D. Reduced cost of cloud resources

13. How does VERSAtileOptic Solutions utilize Terraform's state management feature?

A. To enhance customer support
B. To actively track the state of their cloud resources
C. To increase storage capacity
D. To manage user accounts

14. What advantage does maintaining a history of configurations and modifications in Terraform offer?

A. Easier integration with other tools
B. Improved data encryption
C. Simplified rollbacks
D. Faster data processing

15. What is not a function of Terraform's state management feature?

A. Reflecting the real-time status of resources
B. Enabling easy rollbacks
C. Performance optimizations
D. Managing software updates

16. Which of the following is a correct statement about Terraform's state file?

A. It contains user activity logs
B. It is used for performance optimizations
C. It is irrelevant to infrastructure changes
D. It increases the cost of cloud resources

17. Why is the state file considered a powerful feature in Terraform?

A. It improves the graphical user interface
B. It allows for performance optimizations and precise control over infrastructure changes
C. It manages network security
D. It reduces the need for technical support

18. How does VERSAtileOptic Solutions gain advantages from utilizing Terraform's state file?

A. Increased marketing outreach
B. Active tracking of cloud resources

C. Enhanced physical security

D. Reduced software licensing fees

19. Which of the following commands should be used to update existing resources managed by Terraform to match the current configuration?

A. terraform refresh

B. terraform apply

C. terraform update

D. terraform sync

20. What does the terraform workspace command enable you to do in Terraform?

A. Manage multiple environments with separate state files

B. Perform version control operations

C. Securely store API keys and credentials

D. Validate Terraform configurations

21. What is the first step in using Terraform?

A. Apply the Configuration

B. Initialize the Workspace

C. Run Terraform Plan

D. Test the Exercise

22. What is the role of providers in Terraform?

A. To initialize the workspace

B. To manage and interact with infrastructure resources

C. To apply the configuration

D. To create a simple configuration file

23. Which of the following is not a type of plugin in Terraform?

A. Provider Plugins

B. Provisioner Plugins

C. Custom Plugins

D. Database Plugins

24. What command is used to initialize a Terraform working directory?

A. terraform plan

B. terraform apply

C. terraform init

D. terraform output

25. What are resource blocks in a Terraform configuration file?

A. Commands to initialize the workspace

B. Blocks that define infrastructure objects

C. Commands to apply the configuration

D. Blocks that output variables

26. Which of the following is not a component of a Terraform configuration file?

A. Providers

B. Resources

C. Variables

D. Workspaces

27. What is the structure of a resource block in Terraform?

A. provider, resource, variable

B. resource, attribute

C. attribute, output

D. provider, output

28. How does Terraform manage version control for providers?

A. By using built-in versioning

B. Through external versioning tools

C. By specifying versions in the configuration file

D. Automatically, without user input

29. What command is used to apply the configuration in Terraform?

A. terraform init

B. terraform plan

C. terraform apply

D. terraform output

30. Which of the following is a benefit of using variables and outputs in Terraform?

A. Simplifies initialization

B. Enhances security

C. Increases reusability and modularity

D. Reduces the need for resource blocks

31. What is the primary role of providers in Terraform?

A. To handle user authentication

B. To communicate with APIs of various service providers

C. To install and configure software

D. To manage Terraform's state files

32. What is a prudent step before updating the Terraform codebase?

A. Perform a backup of the current state

B. Delete all resources

C. Rename the configuration files

D. Update all modules to the latest version without testing

33. In Terraform, what is the relationship between plugins and providers?

A. All plugins are providers

B. All providers are plugins

C. Providers and plugins are completely unrelated

D. Plugins and providers are the same thing

34. What is the purpose of a module in Terraform?

A. To handle API requests

B. To perform user authentication

C. To encapsulate pre-configured sets of resources for complex tasks

D. To manage the state file

35. Which type of plugin in Terraform is responsible for tasks like program installation and file uploads?

A. Providers

B. Modules

C. Installers

D. Provisioners

36. What does the AWS provider do when you use Terraform to construct an EC2 instance?

A. It manages the state file

B. It converts HCL code into API requests that AWS can comprehend

C. It performs user authentication

D. It installs the necessary software on the instance

37. Why is Terraform's plugin-based architecture important?

A. It simplifies user authentication

B. It ensures compatibility with all cloud providers

C. It allows for extensibility

D. It automatically manages state files

38. What is not a function of a Terraform provider?

A. Communicating with service APIs

B. Converting HCL code into API requests

C. Handling program installation
D. Offering different kinds of resources

39. Which command would you use to validate the syntax and configuration of Terraform files without executing any actions?

A. terraform plan
B. terraform apply
C. terraform validate
D. terraform refresh

40. What is the primary difference between providers and modules in Terraform?

A. Providers manage state files; modules do not
B. Providers handle user authentication; modules do not
C. Providers communicate with service APIs; modules encapsulate pre-configured resources
D. Providers are not plugins; modules are plugins

41. What is one of the roles of a provider in Terraform?

A. Only API translation
B. Only configuration management
C. Supporting various versions
D. Only resource allocation

42. Which of the following tasks does a provider handle besides supporting various versions?

A. Creating user interfaces
B. Maintaining the status of resources
C. Building databases
D. Designing network topologies

43. What does Terraform init do in relation to providers?

A. Creates a new provider
B. Updates the operating system
C. Downloads the provider plugins
D. Deletes unused plugins

44. Where are the downloaded provider plugins stored within the Terraform configuration directory?

A. In a visible directory
B. In a hidden directory
C. On an external server
D. In a public repository

45. Why is maintaining the status of resources important for a provider?

A. To ensure accurate API translation
B. To manage user permissions
C. To keep track of resource allocation and state
D. To enhance user experience

46. Which of the following is not a responsibility of a Terraform provider?

A. API authentication
B. Supporting various versions
C. Creating user interfaces
D. Maintaining the status of resources

47. What is the purpose of Terraform's remote backend configuration?

A. To integrate Terraform with version control systems
B. To store and manage Terraform state remotely
C. To define encrypted variables for sensitive data
D. To automatically deploy updates to infrastructure

48. How does terraform init contribute to the efficiency of using Terraform?

A. By creating new APIs
B. By downloading necessary provider plugins
C. By deleting unnecessary files
D. By updating the Terraform version

49. When initializing Terraform, what specific action is taken concerning providers?

A. Providers are created
B. Providers are authenticated
C. Provider plugins are downloaded
D. Providers are deleted

50. Which Terraform command is used to import existing infrastructure into Terraform state?

A. terraform state import
B. terraform import
C. terraform add
D. terraform attach

51. What practice does IaC integrate naturally with to provide a comprehensive framework for automating both application development and infrastructure management?

A. Agile Methodologies
B. DevOps Practices
C. Waterfall Method
D. Lean Management

52. When defining a module in Terraform, which block is used to specify required input variables?

A. inputs
B. variables
C. params
D. arguments

53. What is the primary feature of Terraform that makes it suitable for a multi-cloud strategy?

A. Its high cost
B. Provider-agnostic nature
C. Limited support for cloud providers
D. Proprietary language

54. Which command in Terraform is used to show the execution plan before making any changes to the infrastructure?

A. terraform apply
B. terraform init
C. terraform plan
D. terraform destroy

55. What type of file does Terraform use to maintain the current state of managed infrastructure?

A. terraform.state
B. terraform.tf
C. terraform.tfstate
D. terraform.config

56. Which feature of Terraform Cloud or Terraform Enterprise provides visibility into changes made to infrastructure over time?

A. Sentinel
B. VCS Integration
C. State Management
D. Audit Logging

57. What is the purpose of Terraform's count meta-argument in resource blocks?

A. To define how many resources to provision
B. To conditionally create resources based on variables
C. To set dependencies between resources
D. To manage resource lifecycle events

58. Which framework does Terraform integrate with for policy as code practices?

A. Sentinel
B. Vault
C. Prometheus
D. Grafana

59. Which type of backend storage does VERSAtileOptic Solutions use for enhanced security in Terraform?

A. Local storage
B. S3 with encryption
C. Azure Blob Storage without encryption
D. GitHub repositories

60. What is the purpose of using the terraform import command?

A. To export existing infrastructure to a new environment
B. To import existing infrastructure into Terraform state
C. To delete existing resources
D. To initialize the Terraform directory

61. Which command would you use to export the current Terraform state to a file?

A. terraform export
B. terraform state export

C. terraform save

D. terraform store

62. In Terraform, what is the purpose of the depends_on meta-argument in resource blocks?

A. To specify resource dependencies for provisioning order

B. To define input variables for resource configurations

C. To enable conditional resource creation based on variables

D. To enforce resource deletion order during destruction

63. Which file extension is primarily used for Terraform configuration files?

A. .json

B. .yaml

C. .tf

D. .xml

64. What is the role of the Terraform state file `terraform.tfstate`?

A. To store the desired configuration of the infrastructure

B. To maintain a log of all Terraform commands executed

C. To represent the current state of the managed infrastructure

D. To serve as a backup of the Terraform scripts

65. What is the primary advantage of using Terraform's modular design?

A. Reduces the need for version control

B. Facilitates easier management and reusability of infrastructure components

C. Eliminates the need for configuration files

D. Enhances the speed of applying changes

66. You are designing a Terraform configuration that requires dynamic generation of resources based on a variable list. Which construct should you use?

A. for_each
B. count
C. map
D. list

67. Which command is used to initialize a new or existing Terraform configuration?

A. terraform plan
B. terraform init
C. terraform apply
D. terraform destroy

68. How does Terraform handle 'drift' in infrastructure?

A. By manually checking the infrastructure against configuration files
B. By using the `terraform refresh` command to synchronize the state file with real-world infrastructure
C. By applying the configuration changes immediately
D. By storing logs of all changes made

69. What is the purpose of Terraform Workspaces?

A. To manage multiple versions of Terraform
B. To allow collaboration without affecting each other's resources
C. To store sensitive data securely
D. To convert configuration files to JSON format

70. What is 'Policy as Code' in the context of Terraform?

A. Writing policies in the same language as the Terraform configuration
B. Defining and enforcing security policies and compliance requirements as code

C. A feature to convert policies into machine-readable format

D. A method to store policy documents in the state file

71. What is Infrastructure as Code (IaC)?

A. Manual management of IT infrastructure

B. Managing and provisioning IT infrastructure through code

C. A method to write application code

D. A database management practice

72. Which of the following is a key benefit of IaC?

A. Increased manual intervention

B. Higher operational costs

C. Improved disaster recovery

D. Unique setups for each environment

73. What is the primary purpose of Terraform's state file?

A. To store application code

B. To represent the current state of the managed infrastructure

C. To document team meetings

D. To manage user permissions

74. Which command is used to create an execution plan in Terraform?

A. terraform apply

B. terraform init

C. terraform plan

D. terraform destroy

75. What is the significance of Terraform providers?

A. They manage user access

B. They interact with different cloud services

C. They store state files

D. They execute application code

76. How do Terraform modules contribute to IaC practices?

A. By storing state files
B. By acting as reusable, shareable, and configurable components
C. By documenting team meetings
D. By managing user access

77. Which of the following is a declarative language in Terraform?

A. Python
B. Java
C. HashiCorp Configuration Language (HCL)
D. C++

78. What is the purpose of Terraform's terraform init command?

A. To apply changes to infrastructure
B. To initialize a directory and download provider plugins
C. To destroy the infrastructure
D. To format the Terraform code

79. How do Terraform workspaces facilitate collaboration?

A. By storing state files
B. By managing user permissions
C. By providing isolated environments to manage configurations
D. By executing application code

80. What is Sentinel in the Terraform?

A. A language for writing application code
B. A Policy as Code framework
C. A cloud service provider
D. A state management tool

81. What should you consider when declaring explicit dependencies for nested modules?

A. Making sure all modules are published to the Terraform Registry
B. Using the depends_on attribute in the child module only
C. Declaring dependencies both in parent and child modules
D. The sequence of modules in the main configuration file

82. What types of plugins does Terraform create separate processes for?

A. Only providers
B. Only provisioners
C. Providers and provisioners
D. None of the above

83. How do plugins maintain communication with the main Terraform process?

A. Through a shared memory space
B. Over an RPC connection
C. Through a file system
D. Via a cloud service

84. Which of the following operations can Terraform invoke within a plugin?

A. Create and read
B. Update and delete
C. Only read
D. Create, read, update, and delete

85. What is the primary purpose of the communication channel between Terraform and plugins?

A. To synchronize time
B. To invoke specific functions within the plugin

C. To share configuration files

D. To manage logs

86. What does RPC stand for in the context of Terraform?

A. Remote Procedure Call

B. Real-time Processing Channel

C. Remote Plugin Connection

D. Resource Provisioning Code

87. How does Terraform handle multiple plugins when a command is executed?

A. It queues them sequentially

B. It creates a separate process for each

C. It combines them into one process

D. It ignores additional plugins

88. Which of the following is not a function that Terraform can invoke within a plugin?

A. Create

B. Update

C. Execute

D. Read

89. Which Terraform feature allows you to define custom policies to enforce rules and constraints on infrastructure configurations?

A. Sentinels

B. VCS Integration

C. Remote Backend

D. Provider Plugins

90. What happens if Terraform needs to manage both a provider and a provisioner?

A. It creates a single process for both

B. It creates separate processes for each

C. It merges them into one plugin

D. It fails to execute

91. Which type of Terraform plugin is used to manage resources on AWS?

A. Provisioner Plugin

B. Provider Plugin

C. Both A and B

D. None of the above

92. What is the primary role of provider plugins in Terraform?

A. To execute scripts on local machines

B. To manage cloud provider resources

C. To clean up resources before destroying them

D. To initialize VMs

93. Which of the following is a type of Terraform plugin?

A. Resource Plugin

B. Provisioner Plugin

C. Script Plugin

D. Initialization Plugin

94. Provisioner plugins in Terraform are used for:

A. Managing cloud resources

B. Executing scripts during resource creation or destruction

C. Defining infrastructure as code

D. None of the above

95. A plugin used to initialize a VM in Terraform is called:

A. Provider Plugin

B. Initialization Plugin

C. Provisioner Plugin
D. Resource Plugin

96. Which cloud providers have their own provider plugins in Terraform?

A. AWS
B. Azure
C. GCP
D. All of the above

97. What is the less common type of Terraform plugin?

A. Provider Plugin
B. Provisioner Plugin
C. Resource Plugin
D. Script Plugin

98. To clean up before destroying a resource in Terraform, you would use:

A. Provider Plugin
B. Provisioner Plugin
C. Initialization Plugin
D. Resource Plugin

99. Provider plugins primarily interact with:

A. Local scripts
B. Cloud provider APIs
C. Remote machines
D. Initialization routines

100. Provisioner plugins can be used during which phases in Terraform?

A. Resource creation
B. Resource destruction
C. Both A and B
D. Neither A nor B

101. Which feature of Terraform allows you to specify the versions of a plugin you wish to use?

A. Plugin Management
B. Version Control
C. Version Management
D. Plugin Control

102. What is the benefit of specifying plugin versions in Terraform?

A. Ensures backward compatibility
B. Reduces deployment time
C. Increases storage capacity
D. Simplifies user interface

103. What type of environment is being deployed?

A. Simple
B. Complex
C. Basic
D. Static

104. How are explicit dependencies typically used in specialized environments like VERSAtileOptic?

A. To manage inter-module communication
B. To manage API readiness and service provisioning
C. To manage variables and outputs
D. To manage logging and monitoring

105. What is Azure used for in the deployment?

A. Storage
B. Networking
C. Machine Learning

D. Database Management

106. What allows VERSAtileOptic to manage diverse components effortlessly?

A. Cloud Services
B. Plugin Architecture
C. Custom Scripts
D. Manual Configuration

107. What do provider plugins handle?

A. User Interface
B. Deployment Time
C. Intricacies of respective services
D. Network Security

108. What can be developed for unique, in-house solutions?

A. Cloud Services
B. Custom Plugins
C. Provider Plugins
D. Manual Scripts

109. What is the primary role of Terraform in managing plugins?

A. Automating deployments
B. Handling network security
C. Allowing version specification
D. Managing user roles

110. What is dependency propagation in nested modules?

A. Auto detection of dependencies in parent modules
B. Child modules inheriting dependencies from parent Modules
C. Parent modules inheriting dependencies from child modules
D. Random allocation of dependencies in nested modules

111. What are the primary phases of the Terraform workflow?

A. Write, Plan, Apply
B. Design, Implement, Review
C. Code, Test, Deploy
D. Create, Review, Execute

112. What is one of the business advantages of the Terraform workflow?

A. Faster hardware procurement
B. Predictable costs
C. Increased manual intervention
D. Higher employee turnover

113. How does Terraform's Plan phase benefit businesses?

A. Helps them understand cost implications
B. Increases the number of errors
C. Delays the deployment process
D. Reduces transparency

114. What does treating IaC as code allow companies to do?

A. Increase hardware requirements
B. Roll back to previous stable versions easily
C. Reduce cloud storage
D. Eliminate the need for backups

115. What is one of the technological advantages of Terraform's Preview feature?

A. Slower error detection
B. Reduced error rate
C. Increased MTTR
D. Decreased system reliability

116. Which of the following industries would find version control most valuable?

A. Retail
B. Regulated industries
C. Hospitality
D. Entertainment

117. What allows Terraform to support agile development methodologies?

A. Long deployment cycles
B. Write-Plan-Apply cycle automation
C. Increased manual coding
D. Predictable maintenance windows

118. Why is Terraform considered cloud-agnostic?

A.   It works only with a single cloud provider
B.   It manages resources across different cloud providers seamlessly
C.   It requires specific cloud-based hardware
D. It is limited to on-premises solutions

119. You need to pass sensitive data (like passwords or API keys) securely to Terraform configurations. Which mechanism should you use?

A. environment variables
B. plain text variables
C. TF_VAR_* variables
D. sensitive input variables

120. What is the core benefit of the Terraform workflow?

A. It offers a standardized and scalable approach
B. It provides custom solutions for each organization
C. It focuses solely on hardware management
D. It eliminates the need for cloud services

121. In the Write Phase of Terraform, which language is used to define infrastructure in code?

A. Python
B. JavaScript
C. HashiCorp Configuration Language (HCL)
D. YAML

122. What is the main purpose of the Plan Phase in the Terraform workflow?

A. To apply the infrastructure changes
B. To visualize the effects of the code before execution
C. To write the configuration code
D. To destroy existing resources

123. Which of the following commands is used to execute a dry run in the Plan Phase?

A. terraform init
B. terraform apply
C. terraform plan
D. terraform destroy

124. In the provided HCL code, what resource is being created?

A. An S3 bucket
B. An RDS instance
C. An EC2 instance
D. A Lambda function

125. Which command is used to execute the changes previewed in the Plan Phase?

A. terraform init
B. terraform apply
C. terraform plan

D. terraform destroy

126. What tag is assigned to the EC2 instance??

A. Name: "VERSAtileOptic-Server"
B. Name: "VERSAtileOptic-Example"
C. Name: "Example-Instance"
D. Name: "VERSAtileOptic-EC2"

127. In which Terraform phase do you define the provider and specify its region?

A. Write Phase
B. Plan Phase
C. Create/Apply Phase
D. Destroy Phase

128. What is the most effective approach to create multiple AWS EC2 instances using both loops and conditionals based on a condition and a list of identifiers?

A. Using for_each with conditionals
B. Using for without conditionals
C. Using count with a static number
D. Using locals without loops

129. How does Terraform ensure transparency and control during the Create/Apply Phase?

A. By hiding the execution plan
B. By automatically applying all changes without user intervention
C. By showing the execution plan again before applying changes
D. By requiring manual resource creation

130. What is the primary benefit of using HCL for Terraform configurations?

A. It is the only language supported by Terraform.
B. It strikes a balance between readability and automation capabilities.
C. It allows for faster execution of Terraform commands.
D. It integrates seamlessly with all cloud providers.

131. What is the purpose of initializing a Terraform working directory?

A. To execute the Terraform configuration files
B. To prepare the directory for execution
C. To delete unnecessary files
D. To upload files to the cloud

132. Which of the following is not a reason for initializing the Terraform directory?

A. Downloading necessary provider plugins
B. Configuring the backend for storing the state
C. Preparing called modules
D. Deleting old Terraform state files

133. What happens to provider plugins during the initialization of a Terraform directory?

A. They are deleted
B. They are downloaded
C. They are updated automatically
D. They are ignored

134. Which component is responsible for storing the Terraform state?

A. Provider
B. Backend
C. Module
D. Configuration file

135. If your Terraform configuration calls other modules, what does initialization do?

A. It ignores them
B. It validates them
C. It downloads and prepares them
D. It deletes them

136. What does initialization validate in your Terraform configuration files?

A. Content of the files
B. Syntax of the files
C. File size
D. File permissions

137. What is the role of the terraform console command in Terraform?

A. To interactively explore resources managed by Terraform
B. To validate syntax and configurations of Terraform files
C. To perform live updates to infrastructure without applying changes
D. To display execution logs of Terraform operations

138. Which of the following is a true statement about Terraform initialization?

A. It can only be done once
B. It is not necessary for small projects
C. It prepares the directory for execution
D. It automatically applies the configuration

139. You are tasked with deploying a highly available architecture in AWS using Terraform. Which command would you use to create an execution plan to verify the proposed changes?

A. terraform plan -var-file=variables.tfvars
B. terraform validate -target=aws_instance.web

C. terraform apply -auto-approve

D. terraform refresh -input=false

140. Why is initialization particularly crucial in Terraform?

A. It speeds up the execution

B. It ensures the directory is prepared correctly

C. It removes syntax errors

D. It directly interacts with cloud services

141. What is the primary purpose of the `terraform apply` command?

A. To generate an execution plan

B. To destroy the infrastructure

C. To implement changes in the infrastructure

D. To check the syntax of configuration files

142. What must you do before Terraform applies the changes?

A. Manually update the state file

B. Type 'yes' to approve the execution plan

C. Delete the current infrastructure

D. Restart the Terraform server

143. What does Terraform update after successfully applying changes?

A. Configuration files

B. Resource groups

C. State file

D. Virtual machines

144. Which operator is used to evaluate two conditions and returns true if both are true?

A. AND

B. OR

C. NOT

D. XOR

145. After applying changes, how can you manually verify the changes in your VERSAtileOptic environment?

A. Check the updated execution plan file
B. Review the terraform configuration files
C. Validate in VERSAtileOptic
D. Use the command `terraform init`

146. Which of the following is not a valid flag for the `terraform apply` command?

A. `-auto-approve`
B. `-parallelism`
C. `-target`
D. `-destroy`

147. What happens to the state file after you apply changes with Terraform?

A. It is deleted
B. It is updated to reflect the new infrastructure state
C. It is ignored
D. It is backed up

148. What is the default behavior if you run `terraform apply` without any flags?

A. It will destroy the infrastructure
B. It will prompt you to confirm the changes
C. It will skip the execution plan
D. It will apply changes to only specific resources

149. Which command allows you to apply changes only to a specific resource?

A. `terraform apply -auto-approve`

B. `terraform apply -target=aws_instance.my_instance`
C. `terraform apply -parallelism=5`
D. `terraform apply "myplan.tfplan"`

150. What is the purpose of the `-parallelism` flag in the `terraform apply` command?

A. To apply changes without approval
B. To specify the number of concurrent operations
C. To target a specific resource
D. To pass variables during the apply phase

151. What is configuration drift?

A. The intentional modification of infrastructure
B. The divergence of the actual state of the infrastructure from its desired state
C. The use of outdated Terraform versions
D. The accidental deletion of resources

152. Which of the following can be a consequence of human error in Terraform configuration?

A. Enhanced security
B. Reduced costs
C. Unintended creation or destruction of resources
D. Improved performance

153. What impact can versioning issues have in a team environment?

A. They ensure consistent configurations
B. They can introduce inconsistencies
C. They prevent configuration drift
D. They reduce security risks

154. What is a key method to minimize the risk of unintended changes in a Terraform-managed environment?

A. Ignoring the execution plan
B. Always using terraform destroy
C. Thoroughly reviewing the execution plan
D. Avoiding version control

155. Why should test environments be used before deploying changes to production?

A. To reduce cloud costs
B. To mimic production setup and test changes
C. To avoid using terraform plan
D. To prevent any changes from being applied

156. How can version control help in managing Terraform configurations?

A. It prevents any changes from being made
B. It allows tracking of changes over time
C. It eliminates the need for backups
D. It automatically corrects errors

157. What is the purpose of using backups and snapshots for critical resources?

A. To increase deployment speed
B. To restore the environment if something goes wrong
C. To avoid using a test environment
D. To reduce the use of version control

158. You need to update an existing Terraform module to include a new resource block. What sequence of commands would you use to apply these changes and verify the execution plan?

A. terraform init, terraform apply, terraform plan
B. terraform refresh, terraform apply, terraform plan
C. terraform plan, terraform apply, terraform refresh
D. terraform init, terraform plan, terraform apply

159. Why is it important to limit permissions in VERSAtileOptic and Terraform setup?

A. To increase the number of possible changes
B. To reduce the scope of changes, minimizing risk
C. To make the environment more flexible
D. To avoid using backups

160. What is the benefit of locking state files in Terraform?

A. It speeds up the apply operation
B. It prevents simultaneous operations that might cause conflicts
C. It allows more users to make changes at the same time
D. It eliminates the need to review execution plans

161. What is the main goal of maintaining consistency in the style and formatting of code in Terraform?

A. To make the code run faster
B. To prevent security vulnerabilities
C. To avoid misunderstandings, mistakes, and collaboration issues
D. To reduce the size of the code

162. Which Terraform utility is used to update Terraform configurations automatically to follow a consistent style and structure?

A. terraform fmt
B. terraform style
C. terraform update
D. terraform auto

163. What is the recommended indentation size in Terraform?

A. One space
B. Two spaces
C. Three spaces
D. Four spaces

164. Why is two-space indentation recommended by Terraform?

A. It makes the code run faster
B. It is a requirement by cloud providers
C. It keeps the codebase readable without taking up unnecessary horizontal space
D. It is the industry standard for all programming languages

165. What happens if the code is inconsistent or poorly formatted according?

A. It will not compile
B. It might result in misunderstandings, mistakes, and collaboration issues
C. It will be rejected by Terraform
D. It will run slower

166. Which of the following is not a benefit of maintaining consistent code formatting?

A. Improved readability
B. Preventing security breaches
C. Reduced collaboration issues
D. Fewer misunderstandings

167. What does terraform fmt specifically update in Terraform configurations?

A. Security settings
B. Execution speed
C. Style and structure
D. Cloud provider settings

168. What is the purpose of using a null value for an optional attribute?

A. To generate an error if the attribute is missing
B. To omit the attribute
C. To set a default value

D. To declare an attribute as mandatory

169. Which of the following elements is not typically part of a resource configuration in Terraform?

A. Name
B. Type
C. Id
D. resource

170. What type of instance is commonly used in a basic AWS EC2 resource configuration?

A. t2.nano
B. t2.micro
C. t3.micro
D. t2.small

171. What is the purpose of verbose logging?

A. To improve system performance
B. To provide extensive information about activities and transactions
C. To reduce storage requirements
D. To enhance user interface design

172. Which environment variable is used by Terraform to manage log levels?

A. TF_VERBOSE
B. TF_DEBUG
C. TF_LOG
D. TF_TRACE

173. What value should be set to the TF_LOG environment variable to get the most detailed logs?

A. INFO
B. TRACE
C. WARN
D. ERROR

174. How can you save Terraform logs to a file for persistent storage?

A. By setting the TF_SAVE_LOGS environment variable
B. By using the TF_LOG_PATH environment variable
C. By specifying a log file in the terraform configuration file
D. By redirecting output to a file manually

175. In the context of VERSAtileOptic, what do verbose logs help you understand better?

A. The graphical user interface of VERSAtileOptic
B. API interactions and resource provisioning details
C. User activities on VERSAtileOptic
D. Network configurations

176. What kind of issues can be debugged by enabling verbose logging in Terraform?

A. Authentication issues
B. Performance bottlenecks
C. Invalid parameters or insufficient permissions
D. All of the above

177. Which of the following log levels provides the least amount of information?

A. DEBUG
B. TRACE
C. INFO
D. ERROR

178. What is indicated by the log entry 'Acquiring lock for state file'?

A. Terraform is initiating a new operation
B. Terraform is updating the state file
C. Terraform is locking the state file to prevent concurrent changes
D. Terraform is deleting the state file

179. What might you expect to see in the logs if there is a performance issue during a Terraform operation?

A. Detailed event tracking for audit purposes
B. Extensive information about user activities
C. The time taken by individual operations
D. Simplified log entries

180. How would enabling verbose logging help if you encounter an error while creating a new instance?

A. It would automatically fix the error
B. It would show detailed logs, exposing underlying issues such as invalid parameters or insufficient permission
C. It would enhance the graphical interface for better understanding
D. It would reduce the time taken to apply changes

181. What is a backend in Terraform primarily used for?

A. Managing user access
B. Controlling the execution of operations like apply and loading the state
C. Managing API calls
D. Configuring network settings

182. You have multiple Terraform environments (e.g., dev, staging, prod) managed with different state files. How can you switch between environments and manage their state effectively using Terraform commands?

A. Use terraform workspace select <workspace>
B. Use terraform state list

C. Use terraform output

D. Use terraform import <address> <id>

183. Which backend does it specifically focus on?

A. Remote backend

B. Local backend

C. Cloud backend

D. Hybrid backend

184. Where does the local backend store the state file?

A. On a remote server

B. On a cloud storage

C. Locally on your PC

D. In a database

185. For what type of projects does the local backend work well?

A. Large-scale enterprise projects

B. Cloud-based projects

C. Practice or smaller projects

D. Machine learning projects

186. What is one of the benefits of integrating CDKTF with Terraform?

A. Eliminates the need for a Terraform installation

B. Adds multi-language support

C. Replaces Terraform entirely

D. None of the above

187. What is the primary disadvantage of using the local backend?

A. It requires internet access

B. It stores state files on a remote server

C. Not suitable for larger projects

D. It is expensive

188. What is the primary risk associated with resource targeting?

A. It is time-consuming
B. It can cause configuration drift
C. It can corrupt the state file
D. It can remove all resources

189. What does the backend control in Terraform operations?

A. User permissions
B. Execution of operations like apply and the loading of the state
C. Network configurations
D. API integrations

190. How does Terraform differ from other IaC tools?

A. It is limited to AWS
B. It is not provider-agnostic
C. It does not maintain state
D. It is multi-cloud and provider-agnostic

191. What is the default backend for Terraform?

A. AWS S3
B. Google Cloud Storage
C. Local backend
D. Azure Blob Storage

192. What file is used by the local backend to store state data?

A. terraform.json
B. terraform.yaml
C. terraform.tfstate
D. terraform.state

193. In what format is the state file stored?

A. XML
B. JSON
C. YAML
D. INI

194. You need to manage a set of infrastructure resources across multiple AWS regions using Terraform. Which command should you use to apply configuration changes to resources in a specific AWS region only?

A. terraform plan -target=aws_region.us-east-1
B. terraform apply -target=module.region1.aws_region.us-east-1
C. terraform workspace select aws_region.us-east-1
D. terraform init -backend-config="region=us-east-1"

195. You want to perform a dry run to validate Terraform configuration files without actually executing any actions. Which command should you use?

A. terraform validate
B. terraform apply -check
C. terraform plan -dry-run
D. terraform refresh -validate

196. What is not required to set up the local backend?

A. Configuration of cloud storage
B. Additional configuration
C. Network setup
D. All of the above

197. Which of the following commands interact with the backend?

A. init, apply, destroy
B. start, stop, restart
C. plan, execute, finalize
D. configure, manage, deploy

198. Where is the state file stored when using the local backend?

A. Remote server
B. Local filesystem
C. Cloud storage
D. Network attached storage

199. You are deploying a multi-tier application using Terraform. The application requires an isolated network for each environment (dev, staging, prod) with different CIDR ranges. How would you structure your Terraform configuration to achieve this?

A. Define a separate VPC module for each environment and pass environment-specific variables.
B. Use a single VPC module with conditional logic to apply environment-specific configurations.
C. Utilize Terraform workspaces to manage separate state files and configurations for each environment.
D. Use AWS CloudFormation templates instead of Terraform to manage VPC creation dynamically.

200. Why is the local backend considered the default backend in Terraform?

A. It is the easiest to set up
B. It is the most secure
C. It is the most scalable
D. It integrates with all cloud providers

201. What is a major concern when storing the state file locally?

A. Data redundancy
B. Data security
C. Data formatting
D. Data migration

202. You are implementing a Terraform configuration that requires dynamic resource provisioning based on a list of names. Which Terraform construct should you use?

A. count
B. for_each
C. map
D. module

203. Which of the following is a limitation of using local backends for storing state files?

A. Increased storage space
B. Higher costs
C. Collaboration issues
D. Better performance

204. Why might local storage methods be problematic for team collaboration?

A. They are too expensive
B. They require more maintenance
C. They can result in conflicts
D. They are less secure

205. What is a preferred storage option over local backends for larger projects?

A. Google Drive
B. Dropbox
C. S3 or Azure Blob Storage
D. Local hard drives

206. What kind of data can the state file contain that raises security concerns?

A. Non-sensitive data

B. Redundant data
C. Sensitive data
D. Temporary data

207. You want to ensure that sensitive data (e.g., passwords, API keys) used in your Terraform configuration remains secure and is not exposed in version control. How should you manage these sensitive variables?

A. Store them in plain text within Terraform configuration files (*.tf).
B. Use Terraform's sensitive attribute for variables to encrypt them at rest.
C. Utilize environment variables to pass sensitive data securely to Terraform configurations.
D. Store them in a separate, version-controlled file alongside Terraform configuration files.

208. You are planning to deploy Terraform configurations across multiple cloud providers (e.g., AWS, Azure, and GCP). What is a recommended approach to managing provider-specific configurations?

A. Use conditional logic (if statements) within Terraform configurations to manage provider-specific settings.
B. Utilize Terraform modules to encapsulate provider-specific configurations and dependencies.
C. Maintain separate Terraform configurations (*.tf) for each cloud provider and environment.
D. Implement cross-cloud provider plugins to unify the management of provider-specific configurations.

209. What is the potential risk of storing the state file on a local machine?

A. Increased processing time
B. Loss of data
C. Exposure to data security risks
D. Higher storage costs

210. You need to review and approve infrastructure changes proposed by Terraform before applying them. Which sequence of commands should you use to accomplish this?

A. terraform plan, terraform apply -auto-approve
B. terraform apply -check, terraform validate
C. terraform refresh -input=false, terraform plan -out=tfplan
D. terraform init -reconfigure, terraform apply -lock=false

211. What is a good starting point for smaller installations or test scenarios in a VERSAtileOptic environment?

A. AWS S3
B. Local backend
C. Google Cloud Storage
D. Azure Blob Storage

212. You are tasked with designing a Terraform configuration for a microservices architecture where each service requires its own set of resources (e.g., ECS clusters, RDS databases). How would you structure your Terraform modules to achieve this while maintaining scalability and modularity?

A. Create a single monolithic Terraform module for all services to manage resources centrally.
B. Implement a separate Terraform module for each microservice to encapsulate its specific resources and configurations.
C. Utilize Terraform workspaces to manage state files separately for each microservice.
D. Use Terraform providers to dynamically provision resources based on service-specific configurations.

213. Where is the state file located when using a local backend?

A. AWS S3
B. Google Cloud Storage
C. In a remote server

D. In the same system where the tasks are run

214. You are deploying infrastructure across multiple environments (e.g., dev, staging, prod) using Terraform. How can you ensure that changes made in the dev environment do not affect the staging or prod environments until approved?

A. Use Terraform workspaces to manage separate state files and configurations for each environment.
B. Implement conditional logic within Terraform configurations to apply changes based on environment variables.
C. Utilize Terraform Enterprise's policy as code to enforce environment-specific rules and approvals.
D. Apply changes manually using terraform apply -target for each environment to control deployment.

215. You are using Terraform to manage AWS infrastructure that requires integration with existing AWS services (e.g., IAM roles, S3 buckets). How should you securely manage access credentials and permissions required by Terraform to interact with AWS?

A. Embed AWS access keys and secret keys directly in Terraform configuration files (*.tf).
B. Use AWS IAM roles for EC2 instances to provide temporary credentials to Terraform.
C. Store AWS credentials in Terraform state files encrypted with a master key.
D. Utilize Terraform's built-in credential management system to retrieve AWS credentials securely.

216. You need to implement Terraform configurations that support blue-green deployments for an application hosted on AWS ECS. What Terraform feature or configuration approach would you use to achieve this deployment strategy?

A. Utilize Terraform's null_resource to define custom deployment scripts for blue-green deployments.
B. Implement AWS CodeDeploy alongside Terraform to manage blue-green deployments for ECS services.
C. Use Terraform's aws_lb_listener to configure Application Load Balancer (ALB) listeners for blue-green deployments.
D. Define separate ECS task definitions and services within Terraform modules and use conditional logic to switch between blue and green deployments.

217. When should you consider upgrading to more powerful backend technologies like AWS S3?

A. When your infrastructure shrinks
B. When your infrastructure expands
C. When you encounter errors
D. When you run out of local storage

218. What should you do before running the plan and apply operations?

A. Initialize Terraform configurations
B. Write error logs
C. Delete the state file
D. Contact VERSAtileOptic support

219. You are troubleshooting a Terraform deployment that is failing due to resource dependency issues. Which Terraform command or option should you use to inspect resource dependencies and resolve the issue?

A. terraform graph
B. terraform refresh -debug
C. terraform state show
D. terraform apply -target

220. Which backend technology is not mentioned as being compatible with VERSAtileOptic?

A. AWS S3
B. Google Cloud Storage
C. Local backend
D. Azure Blob Storage

221. What is the primary role of Terraform's backend integration?

A. Managing cloud resources
B. Managing states
C. Monitoring applications
D. Managing user roles

222. If you are using nested conditionals to decide the AWS instance type based on environment and GPU support, which Terraform feature would you most likely use?

A. local
B. variable
C. output
D. data source

223. What feature is highly recommended but optional when creating an S3 bucket for Terraform state files?

A. Encryption
B. State locking
C. Versioning
D. Load balancing

224. Which AWS CLI command is used to create an S3 bucket for Terraform state files?

A. aws s3api create-bucket--bucket
B. aws s3api new-bucket--bucket
C. aws s3 create-bucket--bucket
D. aws s3 new-bucket--bucket

225. Where should you specify the S3 backend configuration in a Terraform setup?

A. variables.tf
B. outputs.tf
C. main.tf
D. providers.tf

226. You are managing Terraform configurations across multiple regions with different configurations for each region. What is the best practice for structuring your Terraform code to maintain modularity and reuse?

A. Use a single Terraform configuration file with conditional statements to handle different regions.
B. Create separate Terraform modules for each region and include them in a root module.
C. Use Terraform workspaces to manage state files and configuration variables for each region.
D. Store region-specific configurations in environment variable files and reference them in Terraform code.

227. What should you do if you have an existing local state file when initializing the new S3 backend?

A. Delete the local state file
B. Transfer it to the new S3 backend
C. Create a new state file
D. Ignore the local state file

228. What Terraform command verifies that the backend configuration is working as expected after initialization?

A. terraform start
B. terraform init
C. terraform plan
D. terraform check

229. What is the benefit of using cloud storage solutions for Terraform backend integration?

A. Increased computational power
B. Better user interface
C. High degree of reliability and security
D. Reduced cost

230. Which AWS region is specified in the sample program for creating the S3 bucket?

A. us-east-1
B. eu-central-1
C. us-west-2
D. ap-southeast-1

231. You have a Terraform module that needs to be reused across multiple projects. Which of the following is the most effective way to manage this module to ensure consistency and version control?

A. Store the module code in a local directory and reference it with a relative path.
B. Publish the module to the Terraform Registry and use the module source URL in your Terraform configurations.
C. Use a Git repository to host the module code and reference it using the Git URL in the source attribute.
D. Embed the module code directly into the Terraform configuration files (*.tf).

232. What becomes apparent as you scale with the local backend?
A. Increased ease of use
B. Improved security
C. Limitations
D. Enhanced performance

233. What is a recommended action when limitations of the local backend become apparent?
A. Stop using Terraform
B. Transition to a different backend
C. Increase the size of the local backend
D. Ignore the limitations

234. Which API is used to pull current state files from Terraform Cloud?
A. GET /state file
B. POST /state file
C. GET /state/version
D. PUT /state file

235. What must you do to transition to a new backend in your Terraform configuration?
A. Reinitialize your project
B. Restart your computer
C. Reinstall Terraform
D. Rewrite all configurations

236. What does Terraform prompt you to do when you reinitialize your project with a new backend?
A. Delete the existing state
B. Copy the existing state to the new backend
C. Create a new configuration file
D. Update the Terraform binary

237. What is one of the benefits of using the local backend?
A. High scalability
B. Enhanced security
C. Straightforward management of state files
D. Reduced complexity in large deployments

238. How should the local backend be used accordingly?
A. Extensively for all projects

B. Only for large-scale deployments

C. Judiciously, considering its limitations

D. As a backup solution

239. Which aspect is not a limitation of the local backend?

A. Scalability

B. Security

C. User interface

D. Performance

240. What is the local backend considered in a Terraform journey?

A. An advanced tool

B. A foundational building block

C. A deprecated feature

D. A temporary solution

241. What is the first step to integrate drift detection into a CI/CD pipeline?

A. Initializing Terraform

B. Setting up notification alerts

C. Adding Terraform scripts to a version control system

D. Running terraform plan

242. In GitLab CI/CD, where do you add the pipeline configuration?

A. .github/workflows/action.yml

B. Jenkinsfile

C. .gitlab-ci.yml

D. pipeline.config

243. You are configuring a Terraform backend to store your state remotely in AWS S3. Which configuration options are essential to ensure secure and reliable state management?

A. Set bucket and key in the backend configuration and disable versioning on the S3 bucket.

B. Enable state encryption using kms_key_id and configure region, bucket, and key in the backend configuration.

C. Use terraform init -backend-config to specify the backend configuration file and ignore state encryption.

D. Configure bucket, key, and region in the backend configuration and enable versioning on the S3 bucket.

244. Which file extension is recommended for the drift detection script?

A. .py
B. .sh
C. .js
D. .rb

245. What is the purpose of the 'terraform refresh' command in the drift detection script?

A. To apply changes to the infrastructure
B. To initialize Terraform modules
C. To sync the local state with the real-world infrastructure
D. To destroy the existing infrastructure

246. What output indicates that no drift has been detected?

A. "Changes detected."
B. "Infrastructure is up-to-date."
C. "Drift detected."
D. "No drift detected."

247. How is the script made executable in the CI/CD pipeline?

A. chmod +x drift_detection.sh
B. ./drift_detection.sh
C. terraform apply-auto-approve
D. chmod 777 drift_detection.sh

248. What should the CI/CD pipeline do if drift is detected?

A. Automatically apply changes
B. Exit with status 0
C. Exit with status 1
D. Refresh the state

249. What conditional variable is used to decide whether to apply changes?

A. $APPLY_CHANGES
B. $DRIFT_DETECTED
C. $TERRAFORM_INIT
D. $PLAN_OUTPUT

250. What additional step can be added when drift is detected?

A. Initializing Terraform
B. Sending a Slack message or email
C. Running terraform destroy
D. Fetching the latest code from the version control

251. What is the primary focus of secrets management?

A. Storing API documentation
B. Securely storing, distributing, and managing sensitive data
C. Creating Terraform scripts
D. Automating CI/CD pipelines

252. Why is it critical to manage secrets securely in cloud architecture?

A. To improve script readability
B. To avoid data leaks and unauthorized access
C. To reduce deployment time
D. To increase cost efficiency

253. Which method can Terraform use to read environment variables that start with a specific prefix?

A. TF_VAR_
B. ENV_
C. SYS_VAR_
D. CONFIG_

254. What is a basic method to handle secrets in Terraform scripts?

A. Using an encrypted database
B. Setting them as environment variables
C. Writing them in plain text in the scripts
D. Storing them in a separate repository

255. How can you prompt for secret data at runtime in Terraform?

A. Using the `variable` block with the `sensitive` argument
B. Using a `module` block
C. By writing a custom plugin
D. Storing the data in a file

256. Which system can be considered for a robust and production-grade secrets management solution?

A. AWS Key Management System (KMS)
B. GitHub
C. Google Sheets
D. Local filesystem

257. What tool can dynamically inject secrets into a Terraform script?

A. Azure DevOps
B. Jenkins
C. Vault
D. CircleCI

258. What does the sensitive argument in Terraform do?

A. Prevent sensitive data from being stored in the state file

VERSAtile Reads

B. Mark a variable as sensitive but still store it in the state file
C. Encrypt the entire Terraform configuration
D. Automatically redact sensitive information in logs

259. Which of the following is a best practice for storing Terraform state files?

A. Store them in an encrypted S3 bucket
B. Keep them on a local machine
C. Share them via email
D. Print them out for manual review

260. Why is it important to have a well-thought-out secrets management strategy?

A. To ensure a secure, automated, and efficient operation
B. To increase team size
C. To expedite code review processes
D. To reduce the need for encryption

261. You need to automate the deployment of a Terraform configuration using CI/CD pipelines. Which Terraform command should you include in your pipeline script to initialize the working directory and download the necessary providers and modules?

A. terraform plan -out=tfplan
B. terraform apply -auto-approve
C. terraform init
D. terraform validate

262. Which AWS service is recommended for storing encrypted Terraform state files?

A. EC2
B. RDS
C. S3

D. Lambda

263. In the AWS Management Console, what option must you enable to encrypt an S3 bucket?

A. Versioning
B. Access logging
C. Server-side encryption
D. Object locking

264. Which encryption methods can you choose for encrypting an S3 bucket in the AWS Management Console?

A. AES and DES
B. SSL and TLS
C. AWS-managed keys (SSE-S3) and KMS
D. RSA and DSA

265. In the Terraform backend configuration, what does the "encrypt = true" option ensure?

A. The state files will be compressed
B. The state files will be encrypted
C. The state files will be versioned
D. The state files will be archived

266. What additional attribute must be added to the Terraform backend configuration to use a custom KMS key?

A. kms_key_arn
B. kms_key_hash
C. kms_key_id
D. kms_key_path

267. Where should you manage the VERSAtileOptic API key for better security?

A. Hardcoded in Terraform files
B. Stored in plain text on the server
C. Managed using environment variables or AWS Secrets Manager
D. Written on a sticky note

268. You are managing sensitive data such as database passwords and API keys in Terraform. What is the recommended way to handle these sensitive variables securely?

A. Store sensitive data in plain text variables within the Terraform configuration files (*.tf).
B. Use Terraform's sensitive attribute on variables to prevent them from being exposed in the Terraform plan output.
C. Embed sensitive data directly in the Terraform state file to keep it secure.
D. Use environment variables and reference them using Terraform's var interpolation syntax.

269. Which of the following is not a step in setting up encrypted storage for Terraform state files in S3?

A. Create an encrypted S3 bucket
B. Initialize your Terraform directory
C. Create a custom Customer Master Key (CMK)
D. Configure a load balancer

270. What AWS service is used to create a custom Customer Master Key (CMK)?

A. IAM
B. KMS
C. S3
D. CloudWatch

271. What is the simplest backup strategy for local backend state files?

A. Using Terraform Cloud API

B. Manual Copy
C. Using Consul Snapshot
D. Using a Version Control System

272. Which version control system can be used to track changes in your .tfstate file for local backend backups?

A. SVN
B. Git
C. Mercurial
D. CVS

273. What should you do before pushing the .tfstate file to a repository?

A. Delete sensitive data
B. Compress the file
C. Encrypt the file
D. Change file extension

274. Which API can be used to download the current state file from Terraform Cloud?

A. Consul API
B. Terraform CLI
C. Terraform Cloud API
D. AWS API

275. What is the command to back up the state file using Terraform Cloud's API?

A. curl \--header "Authorization: Bearer $TOKEN" \--header "Content-Type: application/vnd.api+json" \
    "https://app.terraform.io/api/v2/workspaces/$WORKSPACE_ID/current-state-version" > backup.tfstate
B. terraform backup \--header "Authorization: Bearer $TOKEN" \--header "Content-Type: application/vnd.api+json" \

"https://app.terraform.io/api/v2/workspaces/$WORKSPACE_ID/
current-state-version" > backup.tfstate
C.   consul snapshot save backup. snap
D. git commit -m "backup state file"

276. What backup mechanism does Consul provide for state files?

A. Git integration
B. Snapshot Mechanism
C. Terraform Cloud API
D. Manual Copy

277. Which command is used for taking a snapshot backup in Consul?

A. terraform snapshot save backup.snap
B. consul snapshot save backup.snap
C. git snapshot save backup.snap
D. curl snapshot save backup.snap

278. What type of scripts can be used to automate local backend backups?

A. JavaScript or Ruby
B. Perl or PHP
C. Python or Bash
D. Swift or Kotlin

279. How can you back up the state files from the Consul KV store manually?

A. Using Terraform CLI
B. Using Consul's API or CLI
C. Using AWS CLI
D. Using Git commands

280. What is the disadvantage of using a Version Control System (VCS) to store .tfstate files?

VERSAtile Reads

A. It is not scalable
B. It does not support encryption
C. It can store sensitive data unencrypted
D. It is too expensive

281. Which feature in Terraform helps in handling sensitive data such as API keys and passwords?

A. Collections
B. Resource Addressing
C. Protected Secret Injection
D. Terraform Functions

282. Which cloud service is used for storage in the deployment?

A. API keys and passwords
B. Lists, maps, and sets
C. Resource addresses
D. Conditional logic

283. How does Terraform help in recognizing and working with individual resources?

A. Protected Secret Injection
B. Resource Addressing
C. Collections
D. Configuration-Based Conditional Logic

284. Which feature in Terraform is crucial for data formatting and manipulation?

A. Collections
B. Resource Addressing
C. Terraform Functions
D. Conditional Logic

285. What can you add to your Terraform setups to incorporate decision-making capabilities?

A. Protected Secret Injection
B. Resource Addressing
C. Terraform Functions
D. Configuration-Based Conditional Logic

286. What can be used to delve into the complex features of Terraform?

A. Collections
B. VERSAtileOptic case study
C. Resource Addressing
D. Terraform Functions

287. Which feature is not included in Terraform's capabilities?

A. Protected Secret Injection
B. Resource Addressing
C. Terraform Variables
D. Configuration-Based Conditional Logic

288. What does the source material emphasize as crucial when working with Infrastructure as Code (IaC)?

A. Knowing how to destroy resources
B. Handling sensitive data safely
C. Understanding resource addresses
D. Using sets and maps

289. What is the purpose of using Terraform Functions?

A. To inject secrets securely
B. To manage resource addresses
C. To format and manipulate data
D. To add conditional logic to configurations

290. What is "secret injection" in Terraform?

A. Hardcoding sensitive data directly into configuration files
B. Safely inserting private information into Terraform settings
C. Deleting sensitive data from Terraform settings
D. Encrypting configuration files

291. Why is hardcoding sensitive information directly into your configuration files considered bad practice?

A. It makes the configuration files too large
B. It makes the configuration files difficult to read
C. It poses security risks and goes against best practices
D. It slows down the Terraform deployment process

292. Which of the following is sensitive data that should not be hardcoded into your Terraform codebase?

A. Variable names
B. API keys for cloud providers

C, Comments

D, Resource names

293. What can result from hardcoding sensitive data and making it accessible to unauthorized individuals?

A. Improved performance
B. Easier configuration
C. Data breaches and illegal access
D. Faster deployment

294. Which HashiCorp product is recommended for secure data storage when handling secret injection?

A. Consul
B. Nomad
C. Vault

D. Packer

295. What is one of the features of HashiCorp's Vault?

A. It only supports static secrets
B. It provides an extensive API for creating new secrets on the fly
C. It cannot integrate with Terraform
D. It does not support secret revocation

296. Which of the following is not a capability of HashiCorp's Vault?

A. Secret rolling
B. Secret revocation
C. Secret leasing
D. Hardcoding secrets

297. You have a Terraform configuration that needs to deploy resources across multiple regions, but you want to avoid duplicating code. How can you structure your Terraform code to handle this efficiently?

A. Use a single module with conditional logic to handle multiple regions.
B. Create a module for each region and include them in the root module with region-specific variables.
C. Use Terraform workspaces to manage separate configurations for each region.
D. Store region-specific configurations in environment variable files and reference them in the Terraform code.

298. What does secret leasing in HashiCorp's Vault refer to?

A. Permanently storing secrets
B. Creating temporary secrets that expire
C. Encrypting secrets at rest
D. Hardcoding secrets in the codebase

299. Can Vault be integrated with existing infrastructure code and Terraform?

A. No, Vault is not compatible with Terraform
B. Yes, Vault is Terraform-compliant
C. Only with limitations
D. Only for storing non-sensitive data

300. What command is used to start a Vault dev server?

A. vault dev-server
B. vault start dev
C. vault server-dev
D. start vault-dev

301. What should you take note of when starting a Vault dev server?

A. The server's IP address
B. The configuration file location
C. The root token displayed
D.   The server's log file

302. Which command is used to authenticate with Vault?

A. vault authenticate [username] [password]
B. vault login [Your-Root-Token-Here]
C. vault auth [Your-Root-Token-Here]
D. vault sign-in [Your-Root-Token-Here]

303. How do you write a secret to Vault?

A. vault kv put secret/VERSAtileOptic api_key="YOUR-API-KEY"
B. vault secret write api_key="YOUR-API-KEY"
C. vault add secret/VERSAtileOptic api_key="YOUR-API-KEY"
D. vault insert secret/VERSAtileOptic api_key="YOUR-API-KEY"

304. Which of the following Terraform function categories is used for mathematical operations?

A. String Functions
B. Numeric Functions
C. Collection Functions
D. Logical Functions

305. What does the `ceil` function do in Terraform?

A. Rounds a number down to the nearest integer
B. Rounds a number up to the nearest integer
C. Calculates the average of a list of numbers
D. Returns the absolute value of a number

306. Which function would you use to fetch specific elements from a list in Terraform?

A. lookup
B. join
C. element
D. substr

307. What does the `base64encode` function do?

A. Encodes data in JSON format
B. Encodes data in Base64 format
C. Decodes data from Base64 format
D. Encodes data in XML format

308. Which function deals with adding time-based values in Terraform?

A. Timestamp
B. Timeadd
C. Dateadd
D. Timeformat

309. What is the purpose of the `upper` function in Terraform?

A. Converts a string to uppercase
B. Converts a string to lowercase
C. Joins two strings
D. Splits a string into a list

310. Which of the following is a logical function in Terraform?

A. abs
B. and
C. join
D. format

311. What type of expressions does Terraform support for conditional logic?

A. Loop expressions
B. Conditional expressions
C. Iterative expressions
D. Recursive expressions

312. How is a conditional expression formatted in Terraform?

A. condition ? false_val : true_val
B. condition < true_val > false_val
C. condition ? true_val : false_val
D. condition ? true_val > false_val

313. What is the primary purpose of using variables in Terraform modules?

A. To reduce the amount of code
B. To make modules more customizable and manageable
C. To increase execution speed
D. To add comments to the code

314. In the variable block for "security_group_rules," which attribute is not part of the object?

A. Type
B. from_port
C. Protocol
D. size

315. What is the purpose of validation rules in Terraform variables?

A. To format the output
B. To ensure the quality and correctness of input values
C. To enhance performance
D. To add comments to the code

316. How can environmental variables be used in Terraform?

A. To define new resources
B. To populate Terraform variables
C. To delete existing resources
D. To format Terraform scripts

317. Which of the following is the correct way to refer to an environmental variable for a Terraform variable named "name"?

A. TF_VAR_name
B. TF_VAR.NAME
C. TFVARNAME
D. TF_VAR-NAME

318. What variable is checked in the conditional expression to determine the subnet?

A. var.region
B. var.subnet_id
C. var. environment

D. var.instance_type

319. What will the conditional expression return if var.environment is "production"?

A. aws_subnet.prod.id
B. aws_subnet.dev.id
C. var.environment
D. None of the above

320. What is the primary purpose of using a conditional expression in Terraform?

A. To iterate over a list of resources
B. To apply a configuration based on a condition
C. To define a new resource
D. To destroy existing infrastructure

321. What is one of the main reasons for creating custom modules in Terraform?

A. To reduce the number of lines of code
B. To integrate with proprietary software
C. To simplify user interfaces
D. To minimize cloud costs

322. What is a key advantage of using custom modules in Terraform?

A. Faster execution times
B. Improved graphical interfaces
C. Encapsulation of internal best practices
D. Free updates from the community

323. You want to manage Terraform state remotely with version control and collaboration. Which backend configuration is suitable for this purpose?

A. Local backend with a state.tf file

B. S3 backend with state encryption and versioning enabled

C. Git backend to store state in a version-controlled repository

D. Azure Blob Storage backend with a terraform.tfstate file

324. What command would you use to create a backup of your .tfstate file locally?

  A. terraform backup
  B. terraform state backup
  C. Manual copy of .tfstate file
  D. terraform state mv

325. What does the `locals` block in the given code snippet define?

A. Resource configurations

B. Conditional logic

C. Variable types

D. Environment configurations

326. What is the key-value pair in the `common_tags` local?

A.   "Owner" = "VERSAtileOptic"

B.   "Environment" = "Production"

C.   "Tags" = "common"

D.   "Owner" = "Production"

327. How does the `production_tags` local extend the `common_tags` local?

A. By overwriting it

B. By merging with additional tags

C. By duplicating it

D.   By deleting it

328. What additional tag is included in the `production_tags` local?

A. "Owner" = "VERSAtileOptic"
B. "Environment" = "Development"
C. "Environment" = "Production"
D. "Tags" = "Production"

329. What conditional operator is used to assign tags to the `aws_instance` resource?

A. &&
B. ||
C. ?
D. ==

330. When are `production_tags` used for the resource?

A. Always
B. When the environment variable is "production"
C. When the environment variable is "development"
D. When there are no tags defined

331. What is the purpose of defining `local.common_tags` in the code?

A. To create a set of tags for all environments
B. To create tags specifically for production
C. To create tags specifically for development
D. To create tags for testing

332. What should the value of `var.environment` be to use `local.common_tags` for the resource?

A. "production"
B. "development"
C. "testing"
D. Any value other than "production"

333. Which of the following is true about the `locals` block in the given code snippet?

A. It is used to define resource types
B. It is used to define reusable logic
C. It is used to define variable types
D. It is used to define provider configurations

334. What is the standard file extension for a Terraform variable definition file?

A. .tfvars
B. .tf
C. .terraform
D. .var

335. You need to manage Terraform state remotely to facilitate collaboration and version control. Which backend configuration option is suitable for this purpose?

A. local backend with a state.tf file
B. s3 backend with versioning and encryption enabled
C. git backend to store state in a version-controlled repository
D. azure backend with a terraform.tfstate file

336. In the context of VERSAtileOptic, what does environment isolation primarily aim to achieve?

A. Cost-saving
B. Risk containment
C. Code reusability
D. Performance optimization

337. Which approach would allow you to share state files between different environments?

A. Separate Directories
B. Isolated Workspaces
C. Both A and B
D. Neither A nor B

338. What aspect does vertical scaling address in a VERSAtileOptic environment?

A.   Increasing the number of instances
B.   Improving the capability of a single instance
C.   Decreasing the number of instances
D.   Networking optimization

339. You are designing a Terraform configuration that requires conditional logic based on environment variables. Which Terraform feature should you use to implement this?

A. if-else statements in Terraform configuration files (*.tf)
B. for_each meta-argument in resource blocks
C. locals block to define computed variables
D. count meta-argument in resource blocks

340. You are troubleshooting a Terraform deployment issue related to resource dependencies. Which Terraform command should you use to view detailed information about a specific resource's current state?

A. terraform state show <resource_name>
B. terraform graph
C. terraform refresh -debug
D. terraform output <resource_name>

341. If you have defined an output within a module, how do you access it in your main Terraform configuration?

A.   module.<MODULE_NAME>.<OUTPUT_NAME>
B.   output.<OUTPUT_NAME>
C.   terraform output <OUTPUT_NAME>
D.   module-output.<MODULE_NAME>.<OUTPUT_NAME>

342. Which command allows you to apply a configuration change to only a specific resource?

A. terraform apply – target=resource_type.resource_name
B. terraform plan -target=resource_type.resource_name
C. Both A and B
D. Neither A nor B

343. Which command can be used to manually edit the state file?

A. terraform state pull
B. terraform state push
C. terraform state edit
D. terraform state rm

344. Which environment is the initial point where newly written code or features are tested and approved by developers?

A. Production
B. Staging
C. Development
D. Testing

345. What is the primary focus of the staging environment?

A. Feature development
B. Initial code testing
C. Strict testing and performance fine-tuning
D. Real-time user interaction

346. In the provided Terraform configuration, which variable denotes the type of Amazon Machine Image (AMI) used?

A. Region
B. instance_count
C. ami
D. instance_type

347. How do you create a new workspace called 'staging' in Terraform?

A. terraform workspace select staging
B. terraform workspace new staging
C. terraform init staging
D. terraform apply staging

348. What file would contain the specific variables for the development environment?

A. production.tfvars
B. staging.tfvars
C. terraform.tfstate
D. development.tfvars

349. Which command would you use to apply the configurations in the development.tfvars file?

A. terraform apply
B. terraform plan
C. terraform apply -var-file=development.tfvars
D. terraform workspace select development

350. What tag is used in the Terraform configuration to tie resources back to the workspace?

A. "Region"
B. "Environment"
C. "Name"
D. "Type"

Answers

1. Answer: D

Explanation: Integrating Infrastructure as Code (IaC) into Continuous Integration/Continuous Deployment (CI/CD) pipelines automates code testing, deployment, and provisioning/configuration of infrastructure.

2. Answer: B

Explanation: VERSAtileOptic Solutions is highlighted as benefiting from fully automated deployment pipelines, which streamline their deployment processes using IaC.

3. Answer: B

Explanation: Integration of IaC into CI/CD pipelines reduces the need for manual interventions in infrastructure deployment and management, improving efficiency and reducing errors.

4. Answer: C

Explanation: Community-contributed modules for Terraform are typically found in the Terraform Registry, which serves as a central repository for sharing and discovering Terraform modules.

5. Answer: C

Explanation: Open-source projects enrich the IaC ecosystem by providing reusable components, best practices, and community collaboration, driving innovation and standardization.

6. Answer: C

Explanation: Ansible Playbooks accelerate the adoption of Infrastructure as Code (IaC) by providing pre-built configurations and automation scripts. They simplify infrastructure management by allowing users to define and orchestrate the desired state of their IT infrastructure in a declarative language, ensuring repeatable and consistent deployments.

7. Answer: D

Explanation: Benefits of Infrastructure as Code (IaC) in CI/CD pipelines typically include increased deployment speed, enhanced infrastructure security, and reduced manual interventions. Access to community contributions, while valuable, is not directly listed as a benefit of IaC within CI/CD pipelines.

8. Answer: C

Explanation: Terraform providers are responsible for understanding and interacting with APIs of cloud providers (such as AWS or Azure) to create, modify, and manage infrastructure resources defined in Terraform configurations.

9. Answer: C

Explanation: Community contributions to the IaC ecosystem provide access to pre-built solutions, best practices, and diverse perspectives, accelerating adoption and fostering innovation.

10. Answer: C

Explanation: The landscape of IaC is characterized by rich community contributions and numerous open-source projects, which enhance flexibility, scalability, and collaboration in infrastructure management.

11. Answer: B

Explanation: Terraform's state file maintains the state of infrastructure managed by Terraform. It reflects the current state of resources as they exist in the cloud provider environment, allowing Terraform to understand what infrastructure it manages and track any changes made.

12. Answer: B

Explanation: Maintaining a state file in Terraform enables performance optimizations by allowing Terraform to plan and apply changes more efficiently. It also provides precise control over infrastructure changes, ensuring that only necessary updates are applied.

13. Answer: B

Explanation: VERSAtileOptic Solutions uses Terraform's state management to actively track and manage the state of their cloud resources, ensuring consistency and enabling effective management of their infrastructure deployments.

14. Answer: C

Explanation: Maintaining a history of configurations and modifications in Terraform allows for simplified rollbacks. It enables teams to revert to previous infrastructure states if new changes introduce issues, ensuring stability and reliability.

15. Answer: D

Explanation: Terraform's state management feature primarily handles tracking and managing the state of infrastructure resources, enabling easy rollbacks and providing performance optimizations. Managing software updates is typically handled by other tools or processes.

16. Answer: B

Explanation: Terraform's state file is used to optimize performance by storing the current state of managed resources. It helps Terraform understand what changes are needed to bring the actual infrastructure state in line with the desired configuration.

17. Answer: B

Explanation: The state file in Terraform allows for performance optimizations by enabling efficient planning and execution of infrastructure changes. It also provides precise control, ensuring that updates are applied only where necessary, which enhances reliability and consistency.

18. Answer: B

Explanation: VERSAtileOptic Solutions benefits from Terraform's state file by actively tracking the state of its cloud resources. This capability ensures that they can manage and maintain their infrastructure effectively and accurately.

19. Answer: B

Explanation: 'terraform apply not only applies new changes but also updates existing resources to match the current Terraform configuration. It ensures that the state of infrastructure resources aligns with the configuration files (*.tf).

20. Answer: A

Explanation: 'terraform workspace allows you to manage multiple environments (like development, staging, production) within the same Terraform configuration directory, each with its own state file. This helps in isolating resources and configurations per environment.

21. Answer: B

Explanation: The first step in using Terraform is to initialize the workspace using the `terraform init` command. This initializes various Terraform configurations and prepares the environment for further actions.

22. Answer: B

Explanation: Providers in Terraform are responsible for managing and interacting with infrastructure resources. They abstract the APIs and configurations necessary to communicate with various service providers like AWS, Azure, etc.

23. Answer: D

Explanation: In Terraform, plugins include providers, provisioners, and custom plugins. Database plugins are not a standard type of plugin used directly within Terraform for infrastructure management.

24. Answer: C

Explanation: The `terraform init` command initializes a Terraform working directory. It downloads necessary plugins and modules specified in the configuration files and prepares the working directory for Terraform operations.

25. Answer: B

Explanation: Resource blocks in Terraform configuration files define the infrastructure objects that Terraform manages. They specify which resources (such as virtual machines, networks, databases) should be created and how they should be configured.

26. Answer: D

Explanation: Workspaces in Terraform are not components of a configuration file itself. Workspaces are used to manage multiple environments or configurations within a single directory. Components of a configuration file include providers, resources, and variables.

27. Answer: B

Explanation: A resource block in Terraform consists of the resource type followed by its attributes that define the specific configuration for that resource type. For example, defining an AWS EC2 instance would involve specifying its instance type, AMI, and other attributes.

28. Answer: C

Explanation: Terraform manages version control for providers by allowing users to specify provider versions in the configuration files (`terraform.tf` or using the `required_providers` block). This ensures that Terraform uses compatible provider versions for consistent infrastructure management.

29. Answer: C

Explanation: The `terraform apply` command is used in Terraform to apply the changes defined in the configuration files to the real infrastructure. It creates, updates, or deletes resources as needed to match the desired state defined in the Terraform configuration.

30. Answer: C

Explanation: Using variables and outputs in Terraform increases the reusability and modularity of infrastructure configurations. Variables allow parameters to be reused across configurations, while outputs expose values from the infrastructure for reuse in other configurations or scripts.

31. Answer: B

Explanation: Providers in Terraform are responsible for managing the lifecycle of a resource: create, read, update, and delete (CRUD operations). They communicate with APIs of various service providers (like AWS, Azure, etc.) to manage infrastructure resources.

32. Answer: A

Explanation: Before making changes to the Terraform codebase, it's important to back up the current state file (terraform.tfstate). This ensures that you have a snapshot of the existing infrastructure state in case rollback is necessary.

33. Answer: A

Explanation: In Terraform, providers are a type of plugin. Plugins extend Terraform's functionality to interact with different infrastructure APIs, while provisioners handle tasks on those resources after creation.

34. Answer: C

Explanation: Modules in Terraform encapsulate a set of resources that can be used together to achieve specific infrastructure patterns or tasks. They promote reusability and modularity in Terraform configurations.

35. Answer: D

Explanation: Provisioners in Terraform are responsible for tasks like program installation, file uploads, or other configurations on the resource after it is created. They are used to execute scripts on the remote resource.

36. Answer: B

Explanation: The AWS provider in Terraform translates the HCL (HashiCorp Configuration Language) code into API requests that AWS (Amazon Web Services) can understand. Terraform communicates with the AWS API to create, modify, and manage resources like EC2 instances based on the instructions provided in the Terraform configuration files. This process allows Terraform to automate infrastructure provisioning on AWS according to the defined specifications in the Terraform code.

37. Answer: C

Explanation: Terraform's plugin-based architecture allows users to extend its functionality through providers, provisioners, and custom plugins. This extensibility enables Terraform to support a wide range of infrastructure providers and integration with other tools.

38. Answer: C

Explanation: Providers in Terraform do not handle program installation directly. This task is typically managed by provisioners. Providers focus on managing the lifecycle of infrastructure resources through API interactions.

39. Answer: C

Explanation: terraform validate checks the syntax and configuration of Terraform files (*.tf) for errors without executing any actions. It helps ensure that configurations are valid before applying them.

40. Answer: C

Explanation: Providers in Terraform interact with APIs of infrastructure providers to manage resources, while modules encapsulate a set of pre-configured resources that can be reused across different Terraform configurations.

41. Answer: C

Explanation: Providers in Terraform are responsible for supporting various versions of the APIs of the services they interact with. This ensures compatibility with different API versions released by cloud providers, enabling Terraform users to leverage new features and updates without needing to change their infrastructure configuration.

42. Answer: B

Explanation: Besides supporting various versions, a Terraform provider maintains the status of resources by keeping track of their configuration and state, ensuring consistency and managing updates.

43. Answer: C

Explanation: When you run `terraform init`, it downloads the necessary provider plugins specified in your configuration files. These plugins are stored locally within the `.terraform/plugins` directory in your Terraform working directory.

44. Answer: B

Explanation: Downloaded provider plugins are stored in a hidden directory, `.terraform/plugins`, within the Terraform configuration directory. This directory contains all necessary plugins required for Terraform operations.

45. Answer: C

Explanation: Maintaining the status of resources allows a provider to keep track of resource allocation, configurations, and state changes. This is crucial for ensuring that the actual infrastructure matches the desired state defined in Terraform configurations.

46. Answer: C

Explanation: Creating user interfaces is not the responsibility of a Terraform provider. Providers focus on managing infrastructure resources through API interactions and do not deal with user interface aspects.

47. Answer: B

Explanation: Terraform's remote backend configuration specifies where to store the state file remotely (e.g., AWS S3, Azure Storage, Terraform Cloud). This allows for centralized state management and collaboration in team environments.

48. Answer: B

Explanation: `terraform init` contributes to efficiency by downloading necessary provider plugins, ensuring that Terraform has all required components to manage infrastructure as specified in the configuration files.

49. Answer: C

Explanation: During initialization (`terraform init`), provider plugins specified in the configuration files are downloaded and stored locally. This action ensures that Terraform can communicate with the specified infrastructure providers.

50. Answer: B

Explanation: terraform import is used to import existing infrastructure into Terraform state management. It associates resources from a cloud provider or other infrastructure source with Terraform configurations.

51. Answer: B

Explanation: DevOps Practices Infrastructure as Code (IaC) integrates naturally with DevOps practices, facilitating automation, collaboration, and efficiency across application development and infrastructure management.

52. Answer: B

Explanation: In Terraform modules, the variables block is used to declare input variables that are required to be passed when using the module. These variables allow for customization and parameterization of module configurations.

53. Answer: B

Explanation: Provider-agnostic nature Terraform's provider-agnostic nature allows it to manage infrastructure across multiple cloud providers using a unified configuration, making it suitable for a multi-cloud strategy.

54. Answer: C

Explanation: The terraform plan command in Terraform is used to generate and show an execution plan based on the current configuration and state of the infrastructure.

55. Answer: C

Explanation: Terraform uses terraform.tfstate files to store the current state of managed infrastructure. This file is crucial for tracking changes and ensuring consistency between desired and actual state.

56. Answer: D

Explanation: Audit Logging in Terraform Cloud or Terraform Enterprise provides visibility and tracking of changes made to infrastructure configurations and state files over time. It helps in monitoring and maintaining compliance with organizational policies.

57. Answer: A

Explanation: The count meta-argument in Terraform resource blocks allows you to specify how many instances of a resource to provision based on a numeric value. It simplifies the creation of multiple similar resources in a declarative manner.

58. Answer: A

Explanation: Sentinel Terraform integrates with Sentinel for policy as code practices. Sentinel allows organizations to define and enforce policies across infrastructure deployments managed by Terraform.

59. Answer: B

Explanation: S3 with encryption VERSAtileOptic Solutions uses S3 with encryption as backend storage for Terraform, ensuring enhanced security for storing Terraform state files.

60. Answer: B

Explanation: To import existing infrastructure into Terraform state The terraform import command is used to import existing infrastructure resources into Terraform state, allowing them to be managed and modified using Terraform.

61. Answer: B

Explanation: terraform state export exports the current Terraform state to a JSON file. This file can be useful for auditing, backup, or sharing state information outside of Terraform operations.

62. Answer: A

Explanation: The depends_on meta-argument in Terraform resource blocks allows you to specify dependencies between resources. It ensures that resources are created in the correct order based on their dependencies, especially when one resource depends on another for proper configuration.

63. Answer: C

Explanation: Terraform configuration files primarily use the .tf file extension. These files contain the infrastructure configuration written in HashiCorp Configuration Language (HCL).

64. Answer: C

Explanation: To represent the current state of the managed infrastructure terraform.tfstate file in Terraform represents the current state of the managed infrastructure, including resource attributes and dependencies managed by Terraform.

65. Answer: B

Explanation: Facilitates easier management and reusability of infrastructure components. Terraform's modular design facilitates easier management and reusability of infrastructure components, enabling efficient configuration and deployment of complex systems.

66. Answer: A

Explanation: The for_each construct in Terraform allows the dynamic generation of multiple resource instances based on a map or set of strings. It is ideal for creating resources where each instance can have unique configurations based on variables or data.

67. Answer: B

Explanation: The terraform init command initializes a new or existing Terraform configuration directory, preparing it for use by downloading necessary provider plugins and modules.

68. Answer: B

Explanation: By using the terraform refresh command to synchronize the state file with real-world infrastructure, Terraform handles 'drift' in infrastructure by using the terraform refresh command, which compares the current state of deployed resources with the state described in Terraform configuration files.

69. Answer: B

Explanation: Terraform Workspaces provide isolated environments within the same Terraform configuration, allowing teams to work independently on configurations without interference.

70. Answer: B

Explanation: 'Policy as Code' in Terraform involves defining security policies, compliance rules, and operational guidelines in code format, ensuring consistent enforcement across infrastructure deployments.

71. Answer: B

Explanation: Infrastructure as Code (IaC) refers to managing and provisioning IT infrastructure resources using machine-readable code, enabling automation, scalability, and consistency.

72. Answer: C

Explanation: Improved disaster recovery is a key benefit of Infrastructure as Code (IaC) because it allows for consistent and reproducible deployment of infrastructure configurations, enhancing resilience and recovery capabilities.

73. Answer: B

Explanation: The primary purpose of Terraform's state file (`terraform.tfstate`) is to represent the current state of managed infrastructure resources, tracking attributes, and dependencies managed by Terraform.

74. Answer: C

Explanation: The `terraform plan` command in Terraform is used to generate an execution plan that shows the changes that will be made to infrastructure resources based on the current configuration files.

75. Answer: B

Explanation: Terraform providers enable interaction with various cloud services and infrastructure platforms, allowing Terraform to manage resources through API calls and configurations.

76. Answer: B

Explanation: Terraform modules contribute to Infrastructure as Code (IaC) practices by encapsulating reusable, shareable, and configurable components that simplify and standardize infrastructure management.

77. Answer: C

Explanation: HashiCorp Configuration Language (HCL) is a declarative language used in Terraform for defining infrastructure configurations, specifying the desired state of resources without explicitly detailing the sequence of operations.

78. Answer: B

Explanation: The `terraform init` command initializes a new or existing Terraform configuration directory, setting up the environment and downloading necessary provider plugins and modules.

79. Answer: C

Explanation: Terraform Workspaces provide isolated environments within the same configuration, allowing teams to work on different configurations simultaneously without affecting each other's resources.

80. Answer: B

Explanation: Sentinel is a Policy as Code framework integrated with Terraform, enabling organizations to define, enforce, and automate policies across infrastructure deployments managed by Terraform.

81. Answer: C

Explanation: Declaring dependencies both in parent and child modules ensures that dependencies are explicitly recognized and managed at both levels, maintaining the correct sequence and relationship between resources.

82. Answer: A

Explanation: Terraform creates separate processes for providers when executing commands that interact with specific cloud or infrastructure services. Providers manage resource lifecycle operations and translate Terraform configurations into API calls for creating, updating, or deleting resources.

83. Answer: B

Explanation: Plugins in Terraform maintain communication with the main Terraform process over an RPC (Remote Procedure Call) connection. This communication protocol enables plugins to handle resource operations, state management, and other interactions defined by the Terraform configuration.

84. Answer: D

Explanation: Terraform plugins support CRUD operations (Create, Read, Update, Delete) for managing resources defined in the Terraform configuration. Plugins handle API interactions with cloud providers or infrastructure services to implement these operations based on the desired state defined in the configuration.

85. Answer: B

Explanation: The communication channel between Terraform and plugins facilitates invoking specific functions within the plugin, such as resource CRUD operations, state management, and configuration validation. It ensures that Terraform can interact with cloud services and infrastructure components effectively during provisioning and management.

86. Answer: A

Explanation: RPC stands for Remote Procedure Call, which is a protocol used for communication between processes.

87. Answer: B

Explanation: Terraform handles multiple plugins by creating a separate process for each one to ensure they operate independently.

88. Answer: C

Explanation: "Execute" is not listed as one of the functions Terraform can invoke within a plugin. The functions are create, read, update, and delete.

89. Answer: A

Explanation: Sentinels in Terraform allow you to define and enforce custom policies (e.g., security, compliance) on infrastructure configurations. They provide guardrails to ensure that infrastructure changes adhere to organizational policies and best practices.

90. Answer: A

Explanation: Terraform manages providers (cloud or infrastructure services) and provisioners (local or remote actions) using separate processes. If both are involved in a command (e.g., provisioning resources and configuring them), Terraform coordinates and manages them within the same execution context to ensure consistent resource management and configuration.

91. Answer: B

Explanation: Provider plugins in Terraform are used to manage resources on various cloud providers, including AWS. They interact with cloud provider APIs to create, update, and delete resources defined in Terraform configurations.

92. Answer: B

Explanation: To manage cloud provider resources. Provider plugins facilitate interactions with various cloud platforms' APIs, enabling Terraform to provision and manage infrastructure resources like virtual machines, networks, and storage across different cloud environments.

93. Answer: B

Explanation: In Terraform, plugins are used to extend its functionality. One type of Terraform plugin is the Provisioner Plugin, which is used to execute scripts or commands on resources after they are created or updated. Provisioners can be used for tasks such as bootstrapping, configuration management, or executing arbitrary scripts. Resource Plugin is not a specific type of Terraform plugin; instead, resources are managed within Terraform configurations. Script Plugin and Initialization Plugin are not recognized types of Terraform plugins.

94. Answer: B

Explanation: Provisioner plugins in Terraform are specifically designed to run scripts or commands on resources at specific points in their lifecycle, such as during creation or destruction. This allows users to perform tasks like bootstrapping, configuration management, or any other necessary operations that need to occur when resources are being set up or torn down. Managing cloud resources and defining infrastructure as code are broader functions of Terraform itself, not specific to provisioner plugins.

95. Answer: A

Explanation: Provider plugins in Terraform manage the lifecycle of resources, including the initialization of VMs or other infrastructure components on cloud providers such as AWS, Azure, or GCP.

96. Answer: D

Explanation: Terraform has provider plugins for all major cloud providers, including AWS (Amazon Web Services), Azure (Microsoft Azure), and GCP (Google Cloud Platform). These provider plugins enable Terraform to interact with the respective cloud platforms, allowing users to manage and provision resources across these environments using Terraform's infrastructure as code capabilities.

97. Answer: B

Explanation: While provisioner plugins are essential for executing scripts during resource management in Terraform, they are considered less common compared to provider and resource plugins, which handle the core management and definition of infrastructure resources.

98. Answer: B

Explanation: Provisioner plugins in Terraform can include cleanup tasks in scripts executed during resource destruction. This ensures that resources are properly managed and cleaned up according to defined policies or requirements.

99. Answer: B

Explanation: Provider plugins in Terraform interact with cloud provider APIs to manage resources by translating infrastructure configurations into API calls. They handle tasks such as resource creation, modification, and deletion based on desired state definitions.

100. Answer: C

Explanation: Provisioner plugins in Terraform can be used during both the resource creation and resource destruction phases. They allow for the execution of scripts or commands to perform necessary setup tasks during resource creation or cleanup tasks during resource destruction. This flexibility makes provisioners useful for managing configurations that need to be applied or removed at specific points in the resource lifecycle.

101. Answer: A

Explanation: Plugin Management in Terraform allows you to specify the versions of plugins (providers and provisioners) that you want to use in your infrastructure code. This ensures compatibility and consistency across deployments by locking the versions of plugins to specific releases or ranges defined in your configuration files.

102. Answer: A

Explanation: Specifying plugin versions in Terraform ensures backward compatibility with existing infrastructure configurations and API changes. It helps prevent unexpected behavior or errors during infrastructure provisioning and management.

103. Answer: B

Explanation: The type of environment being deployed is described as "complex" because it involves intricate configurations and possibly spans multiple resources and cloud providers, requiring advanced Terraform features and careful management.

104. Answer: B

Explanation: Explicit dependencies in specialized environments like VERSAtileOptic are used to manage the readiness of APIs and ensure that services are provisioned in the correct order. This helps maintain reliability and consistency in infrastructure deployments.

105. Answer: A

Explanation: In the context of infrastructure deployment, Azure is commonly used for various purposes, including storage solutions such as Blob Storage, File Storage, and managed disk services.

106. Answer: B

Explanation: VERSAtileOptic leverages Terraform's plugin architecture to manage diverse components seamlessly. This architecture supports integration with various cloud providers, allowing VERSAtileOptic to orchestrate complex infrastructures efficiently.

107. Answer: C

Explanation: Provider plugins in Terraform handle the intricacies of respective cloud or infrastructure services by translating infrastructure configurations into API calls. They manage resource lifecycle operations such as creation, modification, and deletion.

108. Answer: B

Explanation: Custom plugins in Terraform allow organizations to develop unique, in-house solutions or integrations tailored to specific infrastructure requirements. These plugins extend Terraform's capabilities beyond standard provider plugins available for major cloud providers.

109. Answer: C

Explanation: Terraform manages plugins by allowing users to specify versions, ensuring compatibility and consistency in infrastructure deployments. This version management capability helps maintain reliability and control over plugin usage.

110. Answer: B

Explanation: Dependency propagation in nested modules refers to child modules inheriting dependencies from parent modules. This means that when dependencies are declared in the parent module, they are automatically passed down to the child modules. This ensures that all resources and modules are created in the correct order based on their dependencies, optimizing the deployment and management of infrastructure in Terraform.

111. Answer: A

Explanation: The Terraform workflow consists of three primary phases: writing infrastructure configurations, planning changes, and applying those changes. In the write phase, you define your infrastructure using Terraform's declarative language, HCL. During the plan phase, Terraform generates an execution plan that outlines what actions will be taken to achieve the desired state specified in your configuration files. Finally, in the apply phase, Terraform executes the planned actions to create, modify, or delete resources as necessary, ensuring your infrastructure aligns with your configuration.

112. Answer: B

Explanation: The Terraform workflow provides business advantages such as predictable costs by allowing organizations to plan infrastructure changes, estimate resource consumption, and optimize spending based on planned deployments.

113. Answer: A

Explanation: The Plan phase in Terraform allows businesses to preview the changes that will be made to their infrastructure before they are applied. This phase generates an execution plan, showing what actions Terraform will take. By understanding the proposed changes, businesses can better assess cost implications, identify potential issues, and ensure that the modifications align with their goals and budgets. This phase helps in reducing errors and increasing transparency, rather than delaying the deployment process.

114. Answer: B

Explanation: Treating Infrastructure as Code (IaC) allows companies to manage infrastructure configurations like software code, enabling easy rollbacks to previous stable versions in case of errors or undesirable changes. This practice supports consistency and reliability in deployments.

115. Answer: B

Explanation: Terraform's Preview feature reduces the error rate in infrastructure deployments by simulating changes and highlighting potential issues before applying them. It improves reliability and minimizes the impact of misconfigurations in production environments.

116. Answer: B

Explanation: Regulated industries, such as finance or healthcare, would find version control valuable in ensuring compliance, auditability, and maintaining stable environments. Version control helps track changes, manage configurations, and enforce governance policies.

117. Answer: B

Explanation: Terraform's Write-Plan-Apply cycle automation aligns well with agile development methodologies by enabling rapid and iterative infrastructure changes. This cycle involves writing infrastructure configurations, planning changes to understand their impact, and then applying those changes in a controlled manner. This automation supports agility by allowing teams to quickly adjust infrastructure as requirements evolve, facilitating faster deployment cycles and reducing reliance on manual coding or lengthy maintenance windows.

118. Answer: B

Explanation: Terraform is considered cloud-agnostic because it can manage infrastructure resources across multiple cloud providers (e.g., AWS, Azure, GCP) using a consistent configuration language. It abstracts provider-specific details, allowing users to deploy and manage resources seamlessly across heterogeneous environments.

119. Answer: A

Explanation: Environment variables provide a secure method to pass sensitive data to Terraform configurations without storing them in plain text. This approach enhances security by keeping sensitive information out of version-controlled configuration files.

120. Answer:

Explanation: The core benefit of the Terraform workflow is its ability to provide a standardized and scalable approach to infrastructure management. It automates provisioning, configuration, and management tasks, ensuring consistency and reliability across deployments.

121. Answer: C

Explanation: The Write Phase involves defining infrastructure in code using HCL, which is designed to be both machine-readable and human-friendly.

122. Answer: B

Explanation: The Plan Phase performs a dry run to reveal what will be added, modified, or destroyed, helping to validate the configuration.

123. Answer: C

Explanation: The terraform plan command is used to perform a dry run to preview the changes that will be made.

124. Answer: C

Explanation: The provided HCL code defines an aws_instance resource, which corresponds to an EC2 instance.

125. Answer: B

Explanation: The terraform apply command is used to execute the changes previewed in the Plan Phase.

126. Answer: A

Explanation: Tags in AWS EC2 instances can be customized, but "Name" tags often include identifiers related to the purpose or name of the instance. In this case, "VERSAtileOptic-Server" is a specific tag assigned to the EC2 instance.

127. Answer: A

Explanation: In the Write Phase of Terraform, you define the provider configuration in your Terraform files (provider block) and specify details such as the provider type (e.g., AWS, Azure) and the region where resources will be provisioned.

128. Answer: A

Explanation: Using for_each allows you to iterate over a map or set of resources based on conditions. This method is flexible and allows you to dynamically create resources based on the values in the map or set, which can include conditions to filter out resources based on identifiers or other criteria. This approach is more versatile and aligned with Terraform's best practices for managing dynamic sets of resources.

129. Answer: C

Explanation: Terraform shows the execution plan (terraform plan) again before applying changes (terraform apply). This ensures transparency by allowing users to review exactly what changes will be made to the infrastructure before confirming and applying them.

130. Answer: B

Explanation: HCL is designed to be both machine-readable and human-friendly, making it suitable for defining infrastructure in a readable and automatable way.

131. Answer: B

Explanation: The primary purpose of initializing a Terraform working directory is to prepare it for execution.

132. Answer: D

Explanation: Initializing the Terraform directory does not involve deleting old Terraform state files. Instead, it primarily focuses on setting up the environment for managing infrastructure, including downloading plugins and configuring state storage.

133. Answer: B

Explanation: During initialization (terraform init), Terraform downloads necessary provider plugins that are specified in the Terraform configuration files. These plugins enable Terraform to interact with cloud providers and manage resources.

134. Answer: B

Explanation: The Backend in Terraform is responsible for storing the Terraform state. The state file contains information about the deployed infrastructure, such as resource metadata and mappings, which is crucial for Terraform to manage and update resources accurately. The Backend determines where and how this state information is stored, which could be in remote storage (like AWS S3, Azure Storage, or Terraform Cloud) or locally on disk. The Provider connects Terraform to the underlying infrastructure API (e.g., AWS, Azure); modules are reusable components of Terraform configurations, and Configuration files (*.tf) define the infrastructure resources and their configuration.

135. Answer: C

Explanation: Initialization (terraform init) downloads and prepares any referenced modules in your Terraform configuration. Modules encapsulate reusable infrastructure components and are fetched and prepared during initialization to ensure they are ready for use.

136. Answer: B

Explanation: During initialization (terraform init), Terraform validates the syntax of the Terraform configuration files (written in HCL). It checks for correct syntax, ensuring that configurations can be properly parsed and executed.

137. Answer: A

Explanation: The terraform console command opens an interactive console where you can query and explore resources managed by Terraform. It allows for testing and evaluating expressions, resource attributes, and data sources in real time.

138. Answer: C

Explanation: The Terraform working directory contains .tf files, which are HCL files defining the infrastructure as code. These files specify resources, variables, providers, and other configurations managed by Terraform.

139. Answer: A

Explanation: terraform plan -var-file=variables.tfvars generates an execution plan based on the Terraform configuration files (*.tf) and variables defined in variables.tfvars. It shows what actions Terraform will take to deploy the infrastructure without applying any changes.

140. Answer: B

Explanation: Initialization (terraform init) is crucial in Terraform because it sets up the environment correctly for managing infrastructure. It downloads necessary plugins, configures state storage, and prepares dependencies, ensuring smooth execution of Terraform commands.

141. Answer: C

Explanation: The `terraform apply` command puts the execution plan into action and aligns the real-world infrastructure with the configuration described in the Terraform files.

142. Answer: B

Explanation: Before Terraform applies changes to your infrastructure, it presents an execution plan outlining what actions it will take. To proceed with applying these changes, you need to review the plan and explicitly approve it by typing 'yes' at the command prompt. This step ensures that you are aware of the modifications Terraform will make to your infrastructure and confirms your intention to apply those changes.

143. Answer: C

Explanation: After successfully applying changes (terraform apply), Terraform updates the state file (terraform.tfstate) to reflect the new state of managed infrastructure. The state file tracks resource attributes, dependencies, and metadata.

144. Answer: A

Explanation: The logical operator `AND` is used to evaluate two conditions and returns true only if both conditions are true.

145. Answer: C

Explanation: After applying changes with Terraform (terraform apply), you can manually verify the changes by validating them directly in the VERSAtileOptic environment. This ensures that the applied changes reflect the expected configuration and functionality.

146. Answer: D

Explanation: The `-destroy` flag is not a valid flag for `terraform apply`; rather, it is used with the `terraform destroy` command.

147. Answer: B

Explanation: After applying changes with Terraform (terraform apply), the state file (terraform.tfstate) is updated to reflect the new state of the managed infrastructure. It includes information about resources, attributes, and dependencies.

148. Answer: B

Explanation: When you run `terraform apply` without any flags, Terraform will, by default, prompt you to confirm the changes it plans to apply to your infrastructure. This confirmation step ensures that you are aware of and agree to the modifications before Terraform proceeds with applying them.

149. Answer: B

Explanation: To apply changes to a specific resource in Terraform, you would use the command `terraform apply -target=aws_instance.my_instance`. This command directs Terraform to apply changes only to the resource named `my_instance` within the AWS provider configuration. It's useful for targeting updates to specific resources without affecting the entire infrastructure configuration.

150. Answer: B

Explanation: The `-parallelism` flag limits the number of concurrent operations Terraform will perform during the apply phase.

151. Answer: B

Explanation: Configuration drift occurs when the actual state of the infrastructure diverges from the desired state as defined in your Terraform files.

152. Answer: C

Explanation: Human error can lead to unintended consequences such as the unintentional creation or deletion of resources in the infrastructure.

153. Answer: B

Explanation: Versioning issues, especially when different team members use different versions, can introduce inconsistencies in the infrastructure.

154. Answer: C

Explanation: Thoroughly reviewing the execution plan (terraform plan) before applying changes helps ensure that only intended modifications are applied to the infrastructure, reducing the risk of unintended changes.

155. Answer: B

Explanation: Test environments allow you to test changes in an environment that closely resembles production, reducing the risk of issues when deploying to production.

156. Answer: B

Explanation: Version control systems like Git help track changes over time, making it easier to identify what may have gone wrong if unintended changes occur.

157. Answer: B

Explanation: Having backups or snapshots of critical resources allows for quick restoration in case of issues during the terraform apply operation.

158. Answer: D

Explanation: To update an existing Terraform module, you first initialize (terraform init) the working directory to download the necessary providers and modules. Then, you generate an execution plan (terraform plan) to verify proposed changes. Finally, you apply the changes (terraform apply) to update the infrastructure accordingly.

159. Answer: B

Explanation: Limiting permissions reduces the scope of what can be changed, thereby minimizing the risk of unintended changes occurring.

160. Answer: B

Explanation: Locking state files prevents simultaneous operations, reducing the chance of conflicts and unintended changes.

161. Answer: C

Explanation: The `terraform apply` command puts the execution plan into action and aligns the real-world infrastructure with the configuration described in the Terraform files.

162. Answer: A

Explanation: The `terraform fmt` command in Terraform is used to automatically update Terraform configurations to follow a consistent style and structure. It ensures that the code is formatted according to Terraform's conventions, making it easier to read and maintain. Therefore, option A is the correct answer.

163. Answer: D

Explanation: In Terraform, the recommended indentation size for formatting code is four spaces. This convention helps maintain consistency and readability across Terraform configuration files.

164. Answer: C

Explanation: Two-space indentation is recommended by Terraform because it helps keep the codebase readable while conserving horizontal space. This choice is more about style and consistency rather than a technical requirement or industry standard across all programming languages.

165. Answer: B

Explanation: Inconsistent or poorly formatted code can lead to misunderstandings among team members, introduce errors, and cause issues during collaboration. While Terraform itself does not "compile" code in the traditional sense, it does parse and interpret Terraform configuration files, and poorly formatted code can lead to readability and maintenance challenges.

166. Answer: B

Explanation: Consistent code formatting primarily improves readability, reduces collaboration issues, and minimizes misunderstandings. Preventing security breaches is not directly related to code formatting but rather to implementing secure coding practices.

167. Answer: C

Explanation: terraform fmt updates Terraform configurations to adhere to a consistent style and structure, such as indentation and formatting rules. It does not update security settings, execution speed, or cloud provider settings.

168. Answer: B

Explanation: In Terraform, using a null value for an optional attribute means that you want to omit that attribute from being set or configured. This allows you to express that the attribute should not be included in the resource configuration, rather than setting it to a default value or making it mandatory. It gives flexibility in defining resource configurations based on specific requirements without forcing unnecessary default values or mandatory declarations.

169. Answer: C

Explanation: In Terraform resource configurations, elements like name, type, and resource are commonly defined, but Id is typically not part of the configuration as it represents the unique identifier assigned by the provider to the resource.

170. Answer: B

Explanation: t2.micro is a commonly used instance type in AWS EC2 for basic computing needs, suitable for small-scale applications and testing.

171. Answer: B

Explanation: Verbose logging is used to provide detailed information about the activities and transactions happening within an application, which can help in debugging and performance analysis.

172. Answer: C

Explanation: Terraform uses the TF_LOG environment variable to manage different log levels such as TRACE, DEBUG, INFO, WARN, and ERROR.

173. Answer: B

Explanation: Setting TF_LOG to TRACE provides the most detailed logs, giving extensive information about Terraform's operations.

174. Answer: B

Explanation: The TF_LOG_PATH environment variable allows you to specify a file path where Terraform will save the logs for persistent storage.

175. Answer: B

Explanation: The VERSAtileOptic, verbose logs show RESTful API calls, request and response headers, body, and status codes, helping to understand API interactions and resource provisioning details.

176. Answer: D

Explanation: Enabling verbose logging in Terraform helps to identify issues during development, such as authentication problems, performance bottlenecks, invalid parameters, or insufficient permissions.

177. Answer: C

Explanation: Among the options listed, INFO provides general information without the detailed context provided by DEBUG or TRACE. ERROR provides information specifically about errors encountered.

178. Answer: C

Explanation: The log entry 'Acquiring lock for state file' indicates that Terraform is locking the state file to prevent concurrent changes, ensuring consistency during operations.

179. Answer: C

Explanation: For performance analysis, the logs will show how much time individual operations are taking, which can help in identifying performance issues.

180. Answer: B

Explanation: Enabling verbose logging would provide detailed logs that can help identify underlying issues, such as invalid parameters or insufficient permissions when encountering an error while creating a new instance.

181. Answer: B

Explanation: The backend in Terraform is essential for managing the execution of operations, such as applying configurations and loading the state.

182. Answer: A

Explanation: terraform workspace select <workspace> allows you to switch between different Terraform workspaces (e.g., dev, staging, prod) to manage separate state files and configurations for each environment. It helps in isolating and managing infrastructure resources per environment.

183. Answer: B

Explanation: The local backend in Terraform stores the state file locally on your machine or workstation. It does not involve remote storage or cloud services.

184. Answer: C

Explanation: The local backend stores the state file on the local filesystem of your computer or workstation where Terraform commands are executed.

185. Answer: C

Explanation: The local backend is suitable for smaller projects or personal use but less suitable for larger or team-based projects.

186. Answer: B

Explanation: CDKTF (Cloud Development Kit for Terraform) extends Terraform by adding support for multiple programming languages (such as TypeScript, Python, and Java) to define infrastructure as code. This integration allows developers to leverage familiar programming languages and their ecosystems while still benefiting from Terraform's infrastructure management capabilities. It does not eliminate the need for Terraform itself, nor does it replace Terraform entirely; rather, it enhances Terraform's usability and flexibility by providing additional language options for defining and managing infrastructure.

187. Answer: C

Explanation: The local backend lacks the scalability and collaboration features necessary for larger projects or teams. It is limited to single-machine use and does not facilitate concurrent state management.

188. Answer: B

Explanation: Resource targeting in Terraform (terraform apply -target) can cause configuration drift by modifying specific resources outside of Terraform's managed state, potentially leading to inconsistency between the desired and actual state.

189. Answer: B

Explanation: The backend controls the execution of operations like apply and the loading of the state.

190. Answer: D

Explanation: Unlike some Infrastructure as Code (IaC) tools that are provider-specific, Terraform supports multiple cloud providers and is designed to be provider-agnostic, enabling consistent management of resources across different cloud platforms.

191. Answer: C

Explanation: If no backend configuration is specified, Terraform uses the local backend by default to store the state file locally on the filesystem.

192. Answer: C

Explanation: The local backend stores the state data in a file named `terraform.tfstate`, which is used to keep track of the resources managed by Terraform.

193. Answer: B

Explanation: The Terraform state file is stored in JSON format. This format is used because it is easy to parse and read both by humans and by machines.

194. Answer: B

Explanation: -target option in terraform apply allows you to target specific resources or modules within your Terraform configuration. By specifying the module and resource path (module.region1.aws_region.us-east-1), you can apply changes to resources in a particular AWS region (us-east-1) only.

195. Answer: A

Explanation: terraform validate checks the syntax and configuration of Terraform files (*.tf) for errors without executing any actions. It ensures that configurations are valid before applying them, serving as a dry run validation step.

196. Answer: A

Explanation: Setting up the local backend does not require configuring cloud storage because it stores the state file locally on the filesystem of the machine where Terraform commands are executed.

197. Answer: A

Explanation: The commands `init`, `apply`, and `destroy` all interact with the backend. `init` initializes the backend, `apply` updates the backend with the new state, and `destroy` removes resources and updates the state.

198. Answer: B

Explanation: The state file (terraform.tfstate) is stored locally on the filesystem when using the local backend.

199. Answer: A

Explanation: Structuring separate VPC modules for each environment allows you to customize CIDR ranges and other configurations specific to each environment. This approach promotes modularity and reusability while maintaining isolation between environments.

200. Answer: A

Explanation: The local backend is the default backend because it is the easiest to set up, requiring no additional configuration or infrastructure. It stores the state file locally, which simplifies initial setup and usage.

201. Answer: B

Explanation: The for_each construct in Terraform allows dynamic resource provisioning based on a map or set of strings. It enables you to create multiple instances of resources with unique configurations based on variables or data, such as a list of names.

202. Answer: C

Explanation: Storing the state file locally can expose you to data security risks because local storage is often less secure than managed cloud storage solutions, which can offer encryption, access control, and other security measures.

203. Answer: C

Explanation: Using local backends can lead to collaboration issues because the state file is stored on a single machine, making it difficult for multiple team members to access and update the state file concurrently without causing conflicts.

204. Answer: C

Explanation: Local storage methods can result in conflicts when multiple team members try to access or modify the state file simultaneously, leading to inconsistent states and potential errors in the infrastructure.

205. Answer: C

Explanation: S3 or Azure Blob Storage are preferred storage options for larger projects because they offer reliable, scalable, and secure storage solutions that support concurrent access by multiple team members, reducing the risk of conflicts and data loss.

206. Answer: C

Explanation: The state file can contain sensitive data such as API keys, passwords, and other confidential information that, if compromised, could lead to unauthorized access and security breaches.

207. Answer: C

Explanation: Storing sensitive data in environment variables ensures that it is securely passed to Terraform configurations without being exposed in version-controlled files (*.tf). This approach enhances security by keeping sensitive information out of configuration files.

208. Answer: B

Explanation: Terraform modules allow you to encapsulate provider-specific configurations and dependencies, promoting reusability and simplifying management across multiple cloud providers. This approach enhances the modularity and maintainability of Terraform configurations.

209. Answer: B

Explanation: Storing the state file on a local machine raises the risk of data loss due to hardware failures, accidental deletion, or lack of proper backups, which can disrupt operations and lead to inconsistencies in infrastructure management.

210. Answer: A

Explanation: terraform plan generates an execution plan to review proposed changes, while terraform apply -auto-approve applies those changes automatically without interactive approval. This sequence allows you to review and approve infrastructure changes before deployment.

211. Answer: B

Explanation: For smaller installations or test scenarios, using a local backend is a good starting point because it is easy to set up and manage without needing additional cloud resources or configuration.

212. Answer: B

Explanation: Implementing separate Terraform modules for each microservice allows you to encapsulate service-specific resources and configurations. This approach promotes modularity, reusability, and easier management of infrastructure resources across a microservices architecture.

213. Answer: D

Explanation: When using a local backend, the state file is stored on the local filesystem of the system where the Terraform commands are executed.

214. Answer: C

Explanation: Terraform Enterprise allows you to define and enforce policy as code to control and automate governance across multiple environments. This includes defining rules and approvals specific to each environment ensuring changes are applied according to organizational policies.

215. Answer: B

Explanation: Using AWS IAM roles for EC2 instances allows Terraform to obtain temporary credentials dynamically. This approach enhances security by minimizing exposure of long-term AWS access keys and secret keys in Terraform configurations, aligning with AWS security best practices.

216. Answer: D

Explanation: Implementing separate ECS task definitions and services within Terraform modules allows you to manage blue-green deployments effectively. You can use conditional logic and Terraform's configuration capabilities to switch between different versions (blue and green) of ECS deployments, ensuring smooth application updates with minimal downtime.

217. Answer: B

Explanation: Upgrading to more powerful backend technologies like AWS S3 is advisable when your infrastructure expands, requiring better management of state files, enhanced security, and collaboration features.

218. Answer: A

Explanation: Before running `terraform plan` and `terraform apply`, you should initialize your Terraform configurations using the `terraform init` command to ensure that all necessary plugins and configurations are properly set up.

219. Answer: A

Explanation: terraform graph generates a visual representation of resource dependencies based on Terraform configuration files (*.tf). This helps you inspect and understand how resources are interconnected, facilitating troubleshooting and resolution of dependency-related deployment issues.

220. Answer: C

Explanation: Local backend is not mentioned as compatible with VERSAtileOptic because VERSAtileOptic typically requires cloud-based backends like AWS S3 or Azure Blob Storage for scalable state management.

221. Answer: B

Explanation: The primary role of Terraform's backend integration is to manage the state files, which track the state of the managed infrastructure and are essential for coordinating and storing the information about resources.

222. Answer: B

Explanation: Nested conditionals for determining AWS instance type based on different factors typically involve using Terraform variables to dynamically set configurations based on conditions.

223. Answer: C

Explanation: Versioning is highly recommended because it helps in keeping track of changes to the state file, allowing you to revert to previous versions if necessary.

224. Answer: C

Explanation: To create an S3 bucket for storing Terraform state files using the AWS CLI, you would typically use the aws s3 create-bucket command. The --bucket option is used to specify the name of the bucket you want to create.

225. Answer: C

Explanation: The S3 backend configuration is typically specified in the `main.tf` file, where the primary Terraform configuration for the project is defined.

226. Answer: B

Explanation: Creating separate Terraform modules for each region allows for modular and reusable code. You can then include these modules in a root module, passing region-specific variables and configurations. This approach enhances maintainability and scalability.

227. Answer: A

Explanation: Before switching to an S3 backend, it is recommended to delete the existing local state file to avoid conflicts and ensure a clean transition.

228. Answer: C

Explanation: The `terraform plan` command generates an execution plan and verifies that the backend configuration is working as expected.

229. Answer: C

Explanation: Cloud storage solutions like S3 provide a high degree of reliability and security, ensuring that the state files are safely stored and accessible.

230. Answer: A

Explanation: The `us-east-1` region is often used in examples and sample programs for creating S3 buckets in AWS.

231. Answer: C

Explanation: Storing the module in a Git repository and referencing it using the Git URL in the source attribute ensures that you can maintain version control and reuse the module across different projects. This method promotes modularity and consistency.

231. Answer: C

Explanation: As you scale, the limitations of the local backend become apparent, particularly in terms of collaboration, security, and scalability.

232. Answer: B

Explanation: When the limitations of the local backend become apparent, it is recommended to transition to a different backend, such as a remote or cloud-based backend.

234. Answer: C

Explanation: This endpoint allows you to retrieve the current state version from Terraform Cloud, providing you with the latest state information for your infrastructure managed by Terraform.

235. Answer: A

Explanation: To transition to a new backend, you must reinitialize your project with the new backend configuration using the `terraform init` command.

236. Answer: A

Explanation: Terraform prompts you to delete the existing state when reinitializing with a new backend to avoid conflicts and ensure a fresh start with the new backend.

237. Answer: C

Explanation: The local backend provides straightforward management of state files on the local filesystem, which can be beneficial for small-scale or test deployments.

238. Answer: C

Explanation: The local backend should be used judiciously, considering its limitations in scalability and collaboration, and opting for more robust backends like cloud storage for larger or team-based deployments.

239. Answer: A

Explanation: Scalability is a limitation of the local backend, as it does not support scaling infrastructure management across multiple environments or team collaboration effectively.

240. Answer: B

Explanation: The local backend is considered a foundational building block in a Terraform journey, suitable for initial setups and small projects before transitioning to more robust backends.

241. Answer: D

Explanation: The first step to integrate drift detection into a CI/CD pipeline is to run terraform plan to compare the current state of the infrastructure with the Terraform configuration and detect any differences (drift).

242. Answer: C

Explanation: In GitLab CI/CD, the pipeline configuration is specified in the `.gitlab-ci.yml` file. This file contains the necessary instructions for GitLab to execute various CI/CD tasks, including building, testing, and deploying your code. By defining the pipeline configuration in this file, you can automate the execution of these tasks whenever changes are made to the repository, ensuring consistent and reliable deployments.

243. Answer: B

Explanation: To ensure secure and reliable state management, you should configure the backend with kms_key_id for encryption, and specify region, bucket, and key. This ensures that the state file is encrypted at rest and stored in the correct S3 bucket.

244. Answer: B

Explanation: The recommended file extension for the drift detection script is `.sh`, which denotes a shell script. Shell scripts are commonly used for automation tasks in CI/CD pipelines due to their flexibility and ease of use. By writing the drift detection script as a shell script, you can leverage common Unix commands and utilities to check for infrastructure drift and take appropriate actions based on the results.

245. Answer: C

Explanation: The `terraform refresh` command is used to synchronize the local Terraform state file with the actual state of the real-world infrastructure. This command ensures that the state file accurately reflects the current state of resources, which is essential for detecting drift. Drift occurs when the actual state of the infrastructure deviates from the state defined in the Terraform configuration. By refreshing the state, you can identify any discrepancies and address them accordingly.

246. Answer: B

Explanation: When running drift detection, if no differences or discrepancies are found between the Terraform state and the actual infrastructure, Terraform will output "Infrastructure is up-to-date." indicating that no drift has been detected.

247. Answer: A

Explanation: The `chmod +x drift_detection.sh` command is used to make the drift detection script executable in the CI/CD pipeline. The `chmod` command changes the file's permissions, and the `+x` option adds execute permissions, allowing the script to be run as a program. This step is necessary to ensure that the CI/CD pipeline can execute the script as part of the automation process.

248. Answer: C

Explanation: If drift is detected, the CI/CD pipeline should exit with status 1. This exit status indicates that an error has occurred, signaling to the pipeline that manual intervention or further investigation is required. Exiting with a non-zero status helps prevent the deployment of potentially inconsistent or incorrect infrastructure states, maintaining the integrity of the environment.

249. Answer: A

Explanation: The conditional variable $APPLY_CHANGES might be used in scripts or pipelines to decide whether changes detected by drift detection should be automatically applied.

250. Answer: B

Explanation: When drift is detected, it's often useful to notify relevant stakeholders. Adding a step to send a Slack message or email can alert team members to investigate and take appropriate actions to resolve the detected drift.

251. Answer: B

Explanation: The primary focus of secrets management is to securely store, distribute, and manage sensitive data, such as API keys, passwords, and certificates. This ensures that sensitive information is protected from unauthorized access and breaches.

252. Answer: B

Explanation: Managing secrets securely is critical in cloud architecture to avoid data leaks and unauthorized access. Secure handling of secrets protects the integrity and confidentiality of sensitive data, preventing potential security incidents.

253. Answer: A

Explanation: Terraform can read environment variables that start with the `TF_VAR_` prefix. This method allows you to pass sensitive information, such as credentials, securely through environment variables.

254. Answer: B

Explanation: A basic method to handle secrets in Terraform scripts is to set them as environment variables. This approach keeps sensitive information out of the codebase and can be securely managed at runtime.

255. Answer: A

Explanation: You can prompt for secret data at runtime in Terraform by using the `variable` block with the `sensitive` argument. This ensures that the sensitive data is not displayed in logs or command-line outputs.

256. Answer: C

Explanation: AWS Key Management System (KMS) is considered a robust and production-grade secrets management solution. It provides secure key storage and management, ensuring that sensitive data is protected.

257. Answer: C

Explanation: Vault is an example of a tool that can dynamically read secrets into a Terraform script. It provides a secure way to manage and access secrets, integrating seamlessly with Terraform for secure operations.

258. Answer: A

Explanation: When marking a variable with sensitive = true, Terraform prevents the value of that variable from being stored in the state file, enhancing security by keeping sensitive data out of persistent storage.

259. Answer: A

Explanation: A best practice for storing Terraform state files is to store them in an encrypted S3 bucket. This ensures that the state files are securely stored and protected from unauthorized access.

260. Answer: A

Explanation: Having a well-thought-out secrets management strategy is important to ensure a secure, automated, and efficient operation. It helps maintain the security and integrity of sensitive data while enabling seamless and secure deployments.

261. Answer: C

Explanation: terraform init initializes the working directory, downloads necessary providers and modules, and sets up the backend. This command should be included in CI/CD pipelines to prepare the environment for subsequent Terraform commands.

262. Answer: C

Explanation: Amazon S3 is recommended for storing encrypted Terraform state files due to its robust security features and support for server-side encryption.

263. Answer: C

Explanation: To encrypt an S3 bucket, you must enable server-side encryption in the AWS Management Console, ensuring that all objects stored in the bucket are encrypted.

264. Answer: C

Explanation: The AWS Management Console allows you to choose between AWS-managed keys (SSE-S3) and AWS Key Management Service (KMS) for encrypting an S3 bucket.

265. Answer: B

Explanation: The "encrypt = true" option in the Terraform backend configuration ensures that the state files stored in the backend are encrypted.

266. Answer: C

Explanation: To use a custom KMS key for encrypting Terraform state files, you must specify kms_key_id as an additional attribute in the backend configuration, identifying the specific key to use.

267. Answer: C

Explanation: For better security, the VERSAtileOptic API key should be managed using environment variables or AWS Secrets Manager rather than being hardcoded or stored in plain text.

268. Answer: B

Explanation: Using the sensitive attribute on variables ensures that sensitive data is not displayed in Terraform plan output, enhancing security. It prevents the exposure of sensitive information during the Terraform operations.

269. Answer: D

Explanation: Configuring a load balancer is not a step in setting up encrypted storage for Terraform state files in S3. The relevant steps include creating an encrypted S3 bucket, initializing your Terraform directory, and creating a custom Customer Master Key (CMK).

270. Answer: B

Explanation: AWS Key Management Service (KMS) is used to create a custom Customer Master Key (CMK) for encrypting data in AWS services like S3.

271. Answer: B

Explanation: The simplest and most straightforward way to back up local backend state files is by manually copying the state file to a secure location. This approach does not require any additional tools or setup and ensures that you have a direct backup of your state file.

272. Answer: B

Explanation: Git is a widely-used version control system that can be used to track changes in your .tfstate file. By committing the state file to a Git repository, you can maintain a history of changes, making it easier to track and revert changes if necessary.

273. Answer: C

Explanation: Before pushing the .tfstate file to a repository, it is crucial to encrypt the file to protect any sensitive information it might contain. This ensures that even if someone gains unauthorized access to the repository, they will not be able to read the sensitive data.

274. Answer: C

Explanation: The Terraform Cloud API provides endpoints that allow you to programmatically download the current state file from Terraform Cloud. This is useful for automating backup processes and integrating with other tools.

275. Answer: A

 Explanation: The `curl` command, with the appropriate headers and URL, is used to back up the state file from Terraform Cloud. The headers include an authorization token and content type, while the URL points to the API endpoint for downloading the current state version. This command saves the state file to a local file named `backup.tfstate`.

276. Answer: B

Explanation: Consul provides a snapshot mechanism that allows you to take a backup of the current state of the key-value store, which can include Terraform state files if they are stored in Consul.

277. Answer: B

Explanation: The `consul snapshot save backup.snap` command is used to create a snapshot of the Consul state and save it to a file named `backup.snap`. This snapshot can be used to restore the state in case of a failure or data loss.

278. Answer: C

Explanation: Automation scripts for backing up local backend state files can be written in various scripting languages such as Python or Bash. These languages are commonly used for automation tasks and can easily handle file operations and interactions with other tools or APIs.

279. Answer: B

Explanation: State files stored in the Consul KV store can be backed up manually using Consul's API or CLI commands. This allows you to export the current state and save it for future restoration.

280. Answer: C

Explanation: One major disadvantage of using a version control system to store .tfstate files is the risk of storing sensitive data unencrypted. Terraform state files often contain sensitive information such as infrastructure details and credentials, and if these files are not encrypted, they can be exposed to unauthorized access if the repository is compromised.

281. Answer: C

Explanation: Protected Secret Injection in Terraform is a feature designed to manage sensitive data securely, such as API keys and passwords. This ensures that sensitive information is handled safely within the infrastructure code.

282. Answer: A

Explanation: API keys and passwords are crucial for authenticating and securing access to various cloud services used in deployments orchestrated by Terraform. These credentials are securely managed to ensure the integrity and security of cloud deployments.

283. Answer: B

Explanation: Resource Addressing is a feature in Terraform that allows users to reference and work with individual resources within their configurations. This feature is crucial for identifying specific resources and managing them effectively.

284. Answer: C

Explanation: Terraform Functions are essential for data formatting and manipulation within Terraform configurations. These functions provide various utilities to transform and manage data effectively.

285. Answer: D

Explanation: Configuration-Based Conditional Logic allows Terraform users to add decision-making capabilities to their setups. This feature enables the execution of different configuration paths based on specified conditions.

286. Answer: D

Explanation: Terraform Functions are essential for handling complex features within Terraform configurations. These functions provide the necessary tools for manipulating data, making decisions, and performing calculations to effectively manage infrastructure as code.

287. Answer: D

Explanation: Configuration-Based Conditional Logic is actually included in Terraform's capabilities, allowing for conditional operations based on certain criteria.

288. Answer: B

Explanation: The source material highlights the importance of handling sensitive data safely when working with Infrastructure as Code (IaC). Ensuring that sensitive information is securely managed is vital to maintaining the security and integrity of the infrastructure.

289. Answer: C

Explanation: The primary purpose of using Terraform Functions is to format and manipulate data within Terraform configurations. These functions provide the tools needed to transform input data into the required format for use in the infrastructure.

290. Answer: B

Explanation: Secret injection in Terraform refers to the process of safely inserting private information, such as API keys and passwords, into Terraform settings. This ensures that sensitive data is securely handled and not exposed in plain text within configuration files.

291. Answer: C

Explanation: Hardcoding sensitive information directly into configuration files is considered bad practice because it exposes sensitive data to potential security risks. This can lead to unauthorized access and breaches.

292. Answer: B

Explanation: API keys for cloud providers are examples of sensitive data that should not be hardcoded into the Terraform codebase. These keys should be handled securely to prevent unauthorized access.

293. Answer: C

Explanation: Hardcoding sensitive data and making it accessible to unauthorized individuals can lead to data breaches and illegal access, compromising the security and integrity of the system.

294. Answer: C

Explanation: HashiCorp Vault is recommended for secure data storage when handling secret injection. Vault is designed to securely store and manage sensitive information.

295. Answer: B

Explanation: One of the features of HashiCorp's Vault is its extensive API, which allows for the creation and management of secrets dynamically. This makes it highly flexible and secure.

296. Answer: D

Explanation: Hardcoding secrets is not a capability of HashiCorp's Vault. Vault is designed to manage secrets securely, not to store them in a hardcoded manner.

297. Answer: B

Explanation: Creating a module for each region and including them in the root module with region-specific variables promotes code reuse and maintainability. This structure allows you to manage configurations for multiple regions efficiently.

298. Answer: B

Explanation: Secret leasing in HashiCorp's Vault refers to the creation of temporary secrets that have a defined lifespan and expire after a certain period, enhancing security by reducing the risk of long-term exposure.

299. Answer: B

Explanation: Vault can be integrated with existing infrastructure code and is compatible with Terraform. This allows for secure management of secrets within Terraform configurations.

300. Answer: A

Explanation: To start a Vault development server for testing and development purposes, you use the command vault dev-server. This command initializes and starts a local instance of Vault with default settings suitable for development.

301. Answer: C

Explanation: When starting a Vault dev server, it is crucial to note the root token displayed, as it will be needed to authenticate and perform operations in Vault.

302. Answer: B

Explanation: The `vault login [Your-Root-Token-Here]` command is used to authenticate with Vault using the provided root token.

303. Answer: A

Explanation: The command `vault kv put secret/VERSAtileOptic api_key="YOUR-API-KEY"` is used to write a secret to Vault under the specified path.

304. Answer: B

Explanation: Numeric Functions in Terraform are used for mathematical operations such as addition, subtraction, multiplication, division, rounding, etc. These functions manipulate numeric data and perform calculations within Terraform configurations.

305. Answer: B

Explanation: The ceil function in Terraform rounds a given number up to the nearest integer. It ensures that any decimal part of the number is rounded up, regardless of its value, to the next whole number.

306. Answer: A

Explanation: The lookup function in Terraform is used to retrieve specific elements from a list or map based on a specified key.

307. Answer: B

Explanation: The base64encode function in Terraform converts a given input string into its Base64-encoded representation. This encoding is commonly used for safely transmitting binary or textual data in environments that require ASCII-only communication.

308. Answer: B

Explanation: The timeadd function in Terraform is used to add a specified duration to a given timestamp. It allows you to perform time-based arithmetic operations, such as adding hours, minutes, seconds, etc., to a timestamp.

309. Answer: A

Explanation: The upper function in Terraform transforms all characters in a given string to uppercase. This is useful when you need to standardize the case of string inputs or outputs within your Terraform configurations.

310. Answer: B

Explanation: The and function in Terraform performs a logical AND operation on its arguments. It returns true if all of its arguments are true; otherwise, it returns false. This function is used for evaluating conditions that involve logical conjunctions.

311. Answer: B

Explanation: Terraform supports conditional expressions for implementing conditional logic in its configuration files. These expressions allow you to make decisions based on conditions, such as using different values or resources depending on the evaluation of a condition.

312. Answer: C

Explanation: In Terraform, conditional expressions follow the format `condition ? true_val : false_val`. This syntax resembles common conditional expressions in programming languages, where `condition` evaluates to either `true_val` or `false_val` based on its result.

313. Answer: B

Explanation: Variables in Terraform modules serve to parameterize and customize the behavior and configuration of the module. They allow reusable modules to adapt to different environments or requirements without hardcoding values, thereby enhancing flexibility and manageability.

314. Answer: D

Explanation: In Terraform, variables in a variable block define input parameters for a module or configuration. Attributes such as `Type`, `from_port`, and `Protocol` are typical attributes for defining security group rules, whereas `size` is not typically used.

315. Answer: B

Explanation: Validation rules in Terraform variables help enforce constraints and ensure that input values meet specific criteria, such as being within a certain range, matching a pattern, or meeting other conditions. This ensures that configurations are correct and reduces errors during deployment.

316. Answer: B

Explanation: Environmental variables can be used to provide values to Terraform variables during execution. They allow external configuration and flexibility without modifying Terraform configuration files directly, making deployments adaptable to different environments.

317. Answer: A

Explanation: When using environmental variables to populate Terraform variables, the convention is `TF_VAR_name`, where `name` corresponds to the Terraform variable name. This format ensures that Terraform correctly interprets and assigns the value from the environmental variable.

318. Answer: A

Explanation: In a conditional expression in Terraform, `var.region` would typically be checked to determine which subnet or resource configuration to use based on the specified region. Conditional expressions allow you to dynamically select configurations based on variables.

319. Answer: A

Explanation: If `var.environment` evaluates to "production" in a conditional expression, the expression would return `aws_subnet.prod.id`. This illustrates how conditional logic in Terraform can dynamically select resources or configurations based on the environment or other conditions.

320. Answer: B

Explanation: The primary purpose of using conditional expressions in Terraform is to apply different configurations or resources based on conditions evaluated during deployment. This flexibility allows Terraform configurations to adapt to varying environments or requirements dynamically.

321. Answer: D

Explanation: One of the main reasons for creating custom modules in Terraform is to minimize cloud costs by encapsulating reusable infrastructure configurations. Custom modules allow for standardized deployments and efficient resource management across different projects.

322. Answer: C

Explanation: Using custom modules in Terraform allows organizations to encapsulate and enforce internal best practices, standards, and configurations. This ensures consistency and reliability across deployments, promoting governance and reducing errors.

323. Answer: B

Explanation: Using an S3 backend with state encryption and versioning ensures that the Terraform state is securely stored and versioned, facilitating collaboration and recovery from accidental changes or deletions.

323. Answer: C

Explanation: In Terraform, the main.tf file typically contains the main configuration for a custom module. This file includes the resource definitions, variables, outputs, and other configurations necessary for deploying infrastructure as defined by the module.

324. Answer: C

Explanation: There is no direct Terraform command specifically designed to create a backup of .tfstate files locally. Typically, administrators manually copy or archive .tfstate files to ensure backup and version control of the infrastructure state.

325. Answer: D

Explanation: The `locals` block in Terraform allows you to define local variables within a module. In the context of the given code snippet, it likely defines environment-specific configurations or values that can be reused within the module.

326. Answer: A

Explanation: The key-value pair in the `common_tags` local is `"Owner" = "VERSAtileOptic"`. Locals in Terraform are used to define reusable expressions or values within a module, such as common tags that can be applied to resources.

327. Answer: B

Explanation: In Terraform, locals can extend or override other locals. The `production_tags` local likely merges additional tags with those defined in `common_tags`, ensuring that specific environment tags supplement the common tags without overwriting them entirely.

328. Answer: C

Explanation: The `production_tags` local includes an additional tag `"Environment" = "Production"`. This tag specifies the environment for resources that use these tags, distinguishing them from resources deployed in other environments.

329. Answer: C

Explanation: In Terraform, the conditional operator `?` is used to assign tags conditionally based on a specified condition. For example, tags might be assigned differently based on whether an environment variable indicates production or development.

330. Answer: B

Explanation: `production_tags` are used for the resource when the environment variable indicates "production". Conditional logic in Terraform allows tags or configurations to be applied selectively based on the environment or other conditions defined in the configuration.

331. Answer: A

Explanation: The `local.common_tags` in Terraform is defined to create a set of tags that are common and can be used across all environments, such as specifying common ownership or project tags.

332. Answer: A

Explanation: To use local.common_tags for tagging the resource, the value of the variable var.environment should be set to "production". This ensures that the common tags defined in local.common_tags are applied consistently across resources in the production environment.

333. Answer: B

Explanation: In Terraform, the `locals` block is used to define reusable expressions or values within a module or configuration. It helps in maintaining clarity and reducing duplication by encapsulating logic that can be reused throughout the configuration.

334. Answer: A

Explanation: The standard file extension for a Terraform variable definition file is `.tfvars`. These files typically contain variable definitions that can be used to assign values to variables declared in your Terraform configuration files (`*.tf`).

335. Answer: B

Explanation: Using an s3 backend with versioning and encryption ensures secure and version-controlled storage of Terraform state files, facilitating collaboration and recovery.

336. Answer: B

Explanation: Environment isolation in VERSAtileOptic (and generally in cloud environments) primarily aims to contain risks by separating different environments (e.g., development, testing, and production). This separation helps prevent issues in one environment from affecting others.

337. Answer: B

Explanation: Isolated workspaces in Terraform allow you to segregate state files for different environments while still using the same configuration files. Each workspace maintains its own state, facilitating environment-specific deployments and management.

338. Answer: B

Explanation: Vertical scaling in VERSAtileOptic (and cloud environments in general) involves increasing the resources (such as CPU and RAM) of a single instance to improve its performance or capacity. It contrasts with horizontal scaling, which involves adding more instances.

339. Answer: A

Explanation: Terraform supports conditional logic using if-else statements in configuration files, allowing you to implement different behaviors based on environment variables or other conditions.

340. Answer: A

Explanation: terraform state show <resource_name> displays detailed information about a specific resource's current state stored in the Terraform state file.

341. Answer: A

Explanation: To access an output defined within a module in your main Terraform configuration, you use the syntax `module.<MODULE_NAME>.<OUTPUT_NAME>`. This allows you to retrieve and use values from the module's output in other parts of your Terraform setup.

342. Answer: C

Explanation: Both terraform apply -target=resource_type.resource_name and terraform plan -target=resource_type.resource_name commands allow you to apply configuration changes to specific resources identified by resource_type.resource_name. These commands are useful for targeted changes without affecting other resources.

343. Answer: C

Explanation: The `terraform state edit` command is used to manually edit the state file of Terraform. This command opens the state file in a text editor, allowing you to make modifications or corrections directly to the state information stored locally or remotely.

344. Answer: C

Explanation: The development environment is where newly written code or features are initially tested and approved by developers before moving to other environments like staging or production.

345. Answer: C

Explanation: The staging environment is primarily focused on performing rigorous testing and fine-tuning performance before changes are promoted to the production environment. It simulates the production environment closely.

346. Answer: C

Explanation: In Terraform configurations, the `ami` variable typically denotes the Amazon Machine Image (AMI) ID or name that specifies the operating system and software configuration for instances launched in AWS.

347. Answer: B

Explanation: To create a new workspace named 'staging' in Terraform, you use the command `terraform workspace new staging`. Workspaces in Terraform allow you to manage multiple environments or configurations within the same infrastructure.

348. Answer: D

Explanation: The `development.tfvars` file would contain specific variables tailored for the development environment in Terraform. This file is used to override or set variable values specific to the development environment configuration.

349. Answer: C

Explanation: To apply configurations using variables defined in the `development.tfvars` file in Terraform, you use the command `terraform apply -var-file=development.tfvars`. This command applies the configuration using variable values specified in the file.

350. Answer: C

Explanation: In Terraform configurations, the "Name" tag is commonly used to associate resources with identifiable names, including tying them back to specific workspaces. This helps in managing and identifying resources within different environments.

VERSAtile Reads

About Our Products

Other products from VERSAtile Reads are:

 Elevate Your Leadership: The 10 Must-Have Skills

 Elevate Your Leadership: 8 Effective Communication Skills

 Elevate Your Leadership: 10 Leadership Styles for Every Situation

 300+ PMP Practice Questions Aligned with PMBOK 7, Agile Methods, and Key Process Groups – 2024

 Exam-Cram Essentials Last-Minute Guide to Ace the PMP Exam - Your Express Guide featuring PMBOK® Guide

 Career Mastery Blueprint - Strategies for Success in Work and Business

 Memory Magic: Unraveling the Secret of Mind Mastery

 The Success Equation Psychological Foundations For Accomplishment

 Fairy Dust Chronicles – The Short and Sweet of Wonder

 B2B Breakthrough – Proven Strategies from Real-World Case Studies

CISSP Fast Track Master: CISSP Essentials for Exam Success

 CISA Fast Track Master: CISA Essentials for Exam Success

 CISM Fast Track Master: CISM Essentials for Exam Success

 CCSP Fast Track Master: CCSP Essentials for Exam Success

 CLF-C02: AWS Certified Cloud Practitioner: Fast Track to Exam Success

 ITIL 4 Foundation Essentials: Fast Track to Exam Success

 CCNP Security Essentials: Fast Track to Exam Success

 Certified SCRUM Master Exam Cram Essentials

 Six Sigma Green Belt Exam Cram: Essentials for Exam Success

 Microsoft 365 Fundamentals: Fast Track to Exam Success

www.ingramcontent.com/pod-product-compliance
Lightning Source LLC
LaVergne TN
LVHW081344050326
832903LV00024B/1303